Munich

5km

chleißheim

to Garching

Straße

berg str.

NEUHERBERG

Ingolstädter

urter Ring

ERTSHOFEN

king

straße

Isar Ring

Ungerer straße

MÜNCHNER FREIHEIT

WABING

Englischer Garten

eopold

KÖNIGS PLATZ

MARIENPLATZ

ISARTOR

GER TOR

s Museum

HAIDHAUSEN

ST.-MARTIN-STR.

SING

GIESING

Chiemgaustraße

Tegernseer

FASANGARTEN

FASANENPARK

Landstraße

S2

UNTERHACHING

TAUFKIRCHEN-U.

U6
KIEFERNGARTEN

Freisinger

Isar

Föhringer Ring

FREIMANN

FREIMANN

Landstraße

Münchner Straße

S3

ISMANING

ISMANING

Fischteiche

NEUHERBERG

UNTERFÖHRING

UNTERFÖHRING

Feringasee

KIRCHHEIM B. MÜNCHEN

JOHANNISKIRCHEN

JOHANNISKIRCHEN

ASCHHEIM

Effnerstraße

U4
ARABELLAPARK

OBERFÖHRING

ENGLSCHALKING

ENGLSCHALKING

DAGLFING

DORNACH

HEIMSTETTEN

Heimstettener See

FELDKIRCHEN

FELDKIRCHEN

BOGENHAUSEN

DAGLFING

RIEM

S6

LEUCHTEN BERGRING

Töginger

BERG AM LAIM

RIEM
Straße

ROSENHEIMER PL.

BERG AM LAIM

OSTBAHNHOF

U1
INNSBRUCKER RING

TRUDERING

Flughafen München Riem
(Munich Riem Airport)

GRONSDORF

EGLFING

HAAR

Michaelibad
(Michaeli Swimming Pool)

RAMERSDORF

Quidestr.

Wasserburger

Landstraße

TRUDERING

HAAR

S4

VATERSTETTEN

VATERSTETTEN

PERLACH

PERLACH

Putzbrunner

U2/5
NEUPERLACH SÜD

WALDPERLACH

Straße

PUTZBRUNN

NEUBIBERG

NEUBIBERG

S1

OTTOBRUNN

OTTOBRUNN

RIEMERLING

HOHENBRUNN

INSIGHT *POCKET* GUIDES

MUNICH

Written and Presented by **Joachim Beust**

INSIGHT
POCKET
GUIDES

Insight Pocket Guide:

MUNICH

Directed by
Hans Höfer

Editorial Director
Andrew Eames

Additional Editor
Cliff Vestner

Production Editor
Gareth Walters

Design Concept by
V. Barl

Design by
Willi Friedrich

© 1993 APA Publications (HK) Ltd

All Rights Reserved

Printed in Singapore by
Höfer Press (Pte) Ltd
Fax: 65-8616438

Distributed in the United States by
Houghton Mifflin Company
2 Park Street
Boston, Massachusetts 02108
ISBN: 0-395-65955-8

Distributed in Canada by
Thomas Allen & Son
390 Steelcase Road East
Markham, Ontario L3R 1G2
ISBN: 0-395-65955-8

Distributed in the UK & Ireland by
GeoCenter International UK Ltd
The Viables Center, Harrow Way
Basingstoke, Hampshire RG22 4BJ
ISBN: 9-62421-512-X

Worldwide distribution enquiries:
Höfer Communications Pte Ltd
38 Joo Koon Road
Singapore 2262
ISBN: 9-62421-512-X

Welcome! My first Munich snapshot dates from the 1950s. There I am on a wide street with blue and white trams, the taste of a *Brezl* — a kind of salty bread twist — in my mouth, feeling....elated. I was visiting the big city with my parents, over from provincial Augsburg for the day.

After this, I had intended my next visit to be a brief interlude, but instead it proved permanent: today I find I've lived in this city for 20 years, as a student, taxi driver, barrister, tour guide, journalist and author.

Why is it the city has me, and so many others, in its grip? 'Munich glows' said Thomas Mann. People from all over the world are drawn here in the expectation of achieving something — success, happiness, illumination. The famous Munich light — even clearer when the mysterious *Föhn* wind sweeps down out of the Alps and the atmosphere becomes transparent — all too often becomes a symbol of vanished illusions. For tourists, however, the *Föhn* heralds good weather.

Everyone who lives here loves showing off their city. For you, I've devised personal journeys that I hope will show it at its best, including the ancient Marienplatz, the massive Residenz, the Deutsches Museum and of course the English Garden, where the Bavarians perform that very un-English habit of removing all their clothes on hot days! In addition, I've arranged 19 different optional itineraries to this city's fascinating nooks and crannies, as well as excursions out to sights like the Ammersee Lake and the fairy-tale castles of King Ludwig. I have also provided you with my own selection of restaurants, shops and special events. At the back of the book is all the practical information you could possibly need.

Painting this portrait of the city wouldn't have been possible without the input of many friends: I would like to thank them all; above all Cliff, who helped to write large sections, Gisela, Alex, Willi and, of course, Niku. — Joachim Beust

C o n t e n t s

A New Bridge (and What It Led To)

The history of Munich began in 1156 with what would probably be referred to nowadays as a terrorist attack: Henry the Lion gave the order for the destruction of the Oberföhring Bridge over the River Isar, the property of the Bishop of Freising, and built a new crossing place which he named *Ze den Munichen,* or 'by the monks', after a small monastic community on his territory. His aim in this undertaking was to claim a share of the customs duties levied on the lucrative salt trade. In 1158, now accepted as the official date of the city's founding, the Emperor gave the blessing of legality to the Duke's act of violence, and Munich was awarded the footing essential for economic development—market rights, the privilege of establishing a market.

In the 15th century the merchant class brought the first flowering of culture to this former monastic community. This period saw the construction of the Frauenkirche (Church of Our Lady), whose twin towers have become the city's symbol, and the Gothic Town Hall, not to be confused with the neo-Gothic building at Marienplatz. Erasmus Grasser's impressive *Morris Dancers,* now in the Stadtmuseum (Municipal Museum), also date from this time.

But the bourgeoisie of Munich could only maintain their economic and political position until the Counter-Reformation, a movement supported by the ruling Wittelsbach family for reasons of power politics, among others. Munich also saw the idea of absolutist rule take shape; the court gained more and more influence over the city's ambience, culture and economy. The economically independent merchant class was joined by the aristocracy, by all manner of civil servants and by the new species of citizen who found employment at court in a wide variety of capacities and whose legal and social status was drawn from the absolutist power of the rulers who supplied that employment. From this stemmed that cautious, don't-rock-the-boat attitude which still characterizes everything touching upon political and economic power in present-day Munich.

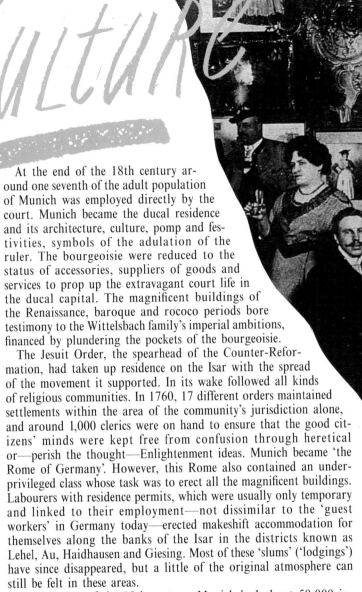

At the end of the 18th century around one seventh of the adult population of Munich was employed directly by the court. Munich became the ducal residence and its architecture, culture, pomp and festivities, symbols of the adulation of the ruler. The bourgeoisie were reduced to the status of accessories, suppliers of goods and services to prop up the extravagant court life in the ducal capital. The magnificent buildings of the Renaissance, baroque and rococo periods bore testimony to the Wittelsbach family's imperial ambitions, financed by plundering the pockets of the bourgeoisie.

The Jesuit Order, the spearhead of the Counter-Reformation, had taken up residence on the Isar with the spread of the movement it supported. In its wake followed all kinds of religious communities. In 1760, 17 different orders maintained settlements within the area of the community's jurisdiction alone, and around 1,000 clerics were on hand to ensure that the good citizens' minds were kept free from confusion through heretical or—perish the thought—Enlightenment ideas. Munich became 'the Rome of Germany'. However, this Rome also contained an under-privileged class whose task was to erect all the magnificent buildings. Labourers with residence permits, which were usually only temporary and linked to their employment—not dissimilar to the 'guest workers' in Germany today—erected makeshift accommodation for themselves along the banks of the Isar in the districts known as Lehel, Au, Haidhausen and Giesing. Most of these 'slums' ('lodgings') have since disappeared, but a little of the original atmosphere can still be felt in these areas.

By the start of the 18th century, Munich had about 50,000 inhabitants—three times as many as at the end of the Thirty Years War—but by the end of the 19th century it had grown to 500,000, the final proof that *Ze den Munichen* had attained the status of a city. However, the combination of bureaucracy and provincialism which characterized the royal seat, until recently so frequently dubbed 'the mega-village', remained largely unaltered.

In the wake of the new Napoleonic order in Europe, those members of the Wittelsbach family who had risen to the rank of

king—Ludwig I, Maximilian II and Ludwig II—had spared no pains to rid the city of its provincialism. Many of the magnificent buildings which are the chief tourist attractions of today date from this period, as indeed does the Oktoberfest, first celebrated in 1810 on the occasion of the wedding of Crown Prince Ludwig.

But the ambitious Wittelsbachs would by no means content themselves with architecture which faithfully echoed its classical models, such as the buildings at Königsplatz. Their aim was to transform Munich into a second Paris, and to this end they enticed artists and intellectuals to the Isar from every corner of Europe, busying themselves with the construction and development of museums, libraries, archives and universities.

These efforts to create an identity for the region's capital met with success, but of a somewhat different type than the one anticipated. The painters, sculptors, poets and intellectuals soon developed a life of their own and broke free from the royal embrace. In the last years of the 19th century this brought them into open conflict with the royal palace and its cultural bureaucracy, a conflict which stimulated their openness and cultural and intellectual richness.

The *Blue Rider*, the *Simplizissimus* and the magazine *Jugend* (Youth), all testified to the current of licence and liberty sweeping the streets of Schwabing. The official and, above all, the deep-rooted, 'traditional' city of Munich was at its wit's end with the wild bunch in *Wahnmoching* (Crazyville), and would have been only too happy to pack off the unwelcome spirits it had summoned right back to where they had come from.

The First World War brought an end to that Golden Age on which the city still prides itself today, when evidence of artistic feeling and freedom of thought is called for in official speeches. In the 1920s Berlin took over as the home of the avant-garde of intel-

lectual and artistic creativity, and Munich sank back into the traditional provincialism which it has been trying to shake off ever since.

Between the wars Munich became the setting for a completely different scene. Adolf Hitler gained political notoriety in the heavy air of the beer cellars and created what the Nazis called 'the capital of the Movement' out of the 'Athens on the Isar'. Königsplatz, where Ludwig I had placed copies of the Propylaea of Athens, became the location of 'the Führer's edifices', and the SS stood guard before Nazi temples whose plinths can still be made out today among the undergrowth. The Haus der Kunst (House of Art), then still bearing the name Haus der Deutschen Kunst (House of German Art), is also a creation of the Nazi era.

The Second World War took a heavy toll in Munich, but a far heavier penalty was exacted by the town planners in the 'Second Demolition'. Their intention of turning Munich into a kind of motorway extension was only partially transformed into reality, and the result can be seen, if not always believed, when driving along the Old Town Ring Road (Altstadtring). But at least now there is talk of banning cars from the city centre completely, and new bicycle paths are the first step in this direction.

The Olympic Games marked a turning point in the city's development. They contributed the Middle Ring Road (Mittlerer Ring), enabling drivers to circumnavigate Munich, but were also the catalyst for the construction of a modern public transport network and truly excellent sports and leisure facilities. Munich is advancing into the 1990s with a

The Hypobank

confidence which comes from having become the most prosperous city in Germany. The status of European metropolis so desired by Ludwig I seems (almost) to have been attained.

Getting Your Bearings

It's not always easy finding your way around Munich. Even taxi drivers have problems now and then. Only the chequerboard layout of Schwabing makes orientation easy. Wandering drivers will find the Mittlerer Ring (Middle Ring Road), clearly signposted, a real lifeline. It's often worth approaching a destination on the other side of the city by driving around the centre rather than through it, although this should not be attempted in the evening rush hour, when traffic jams on Petueslring are the norm.

Other important aids to orientation are the River Isar and Leopold/Ludwigstraße from the north, and the railway lines from the Hauptbahnhof to the east. From the east, Prinzregentenstraße and Rosenheimer Straße, and from the south, Albert-Roßhaupter/Lindwurmstraße, are the simplest routes into town.

The Isar flows through some of Munich's most fascinating areas. South from Kennedy Bridge to Baldeplatz, stretches of idyllic park alternate with residential areas along both banks. The Deutsches Museum on the Isar Island is only a stone's throw from Isartor and the city centre.

Westwards from the Hauptbahnhof to Pasing, towards the Stuttgart motorway, the railway tracks and Landsberger Straße divide Neuhausen/Nymphenburg from Westend and Laim. Of particular interest to tourists is the north-south axis of Leopold/Ludwigstraße, which ends at the Feldherrenhalle and runs into the shopping paradise of Theatinerstraße. This street runs through Schwabing past Maxvorstadt and the university. The Siegestor, the State Library and other sights lie along its route, and it's not far to the English Garden. This is also a quick route out of town.

Most hotels are concentrated around the Hauptbahnhof, where you can also find Munich's prim but expensive red light and rip-off district. The big hotel chains have opened on both sides of the Isar, and the two top hotels, the Bayerischer Hof and the Hotel Vier Jahreszeiten, are on the Maximilian/Perusa/Maffeistraße axis, on the edge of the city centre.

Munich's Franz Josef Strauß Airport at Erding, opened in May 1992, is a mere 40 minutes from the city centre on the motorways to Nürnberg (A9) or Deggendorf (A92). But these routes are prone to delays, so be pessimistic when calculating your journey time.

The airport can also be reached by public transport (S8) which will take about the same time. Taxis cost about DM100.

Historical Highlights

BC

15 Rome annexes Bavaria as the Province of Rhaetia, with Augsburg as the capital.

AD

From 475 Baiuvarii and Boii found settlements.

739 Diocese of Freising founded by Saint Corbinian.

10th century Monks from Tegernsee settle on the Isar.

1156 Henry the Lion (ruler 1156–80) destroys episcopal bridge over the Isar.

1158 Official date of city's foundation. Munich awarded market, customs and coinage rights.

1328 Ludwig IV (the Bavarian) proclaimed Emperor of Germany. Munich becomes capital of Holy Roman Empire of the German Nation.

1468–88 Construction of late Gothic Frauenkirche (Cathedral).

1550–79 Duke Albrecht V introduces Renaissance pomp and glory to Munich life.

1618–48 Thirty Years War; town occupied by Swedish army. Maximilian I forced to flee.

From 1680 The baroque dominates Munich architecture.

1705–15 During Spanish War of Succession, Bavaria signs treaty with France and is occupied by the Austrians.

1799–1825 Maximilian IV Joseph extends Bavaria's old boundaries to include Swabian and Franconian territory.

1805 Napoleon in Munich.

1806 Napoleon appoints Maximilian IV Joseph as first Bavarian king.

1810 Wedding of Crown Prince Ludwig, 12 October; every year since, the Oktoberfest has taken place on Theresienwiese.

1825–48 King Ludwig I introduces classicism into architecture; adopts role of generous patron of the arts. Scandal with Lola Montez. He abdicates during 1848 revolution.

1864–86 Rule of Ludwig II, the most famous and eccentric Bavarian king, characterized by his bizarre lifestyle, building mania (Neuschwanstein, Linderhof, Herrenchiemsee castles), and pathological love for Wagner. He died under mysterious circumstances in Starnberger See.

1886–1912 Prince Rupert Luitpold, son of Ludwig I, rules in place of the mentally unstable Otto I.,brother of Ludwig II.

1913–18 Rule of Ludwig III, last member of Bavaria's constitutional monarchy.

1918 On 8 November, Kurt Eisner, leader of the USPD (Independent Social Democrats), proclaims Bavaria a free state after a workers' uprising in the period of hardship following the war.

1919 USPD defeated, Eisner murdered, short-lived Soviet republic proclaimed.

1923 Hitler's putsch in Bürgerbräukeller, Rosenheimer Berg.

1933 Munich becomes 'Capital of the Movement'. Father Rupert Mayer preaches sermons of resistance.

1938 Munich Agreement.

1943 Resistance movement formed at Munich University by Scholls and Professor Huber under the code name 'White Rose'.

1945 On 30 April occupying forces of the US army move into the city, 70 percent of which has been destroyed.

1946 Bavaria receives constitution, still in force today.

1948-60 Rebuilding of Munich.

1972 Olympic Games.

1990 Red-Green majority on City Council. Unification of Germany under Helmut Kohl.

The Great Germanic Dream Machine

There's a buzz word on everyone's lips these days which determines
the worth of individuals, businesses—even cities: image. Image seems
to be everything, and Munich has bought into the concept whole-
heartedly; so much so that boosters of the Bavarian capital sometimes
no longer distinguish between fact and fiction. Munich today walks
a tightrope between the image outsiders project upon it and its own
perception of itself.

Fact: Munich is Germany's number one fashion, fair and conference
city. Fact: no other city produces so many films or TV programmes.
Fact: site of the world's largest museum of science and technology, it
is also the beer capital of the world, home of the largest green area
in a city in Europe, etc, etc.

Meanwhile, back in reality, the city's residents attempt to live a
normal life and resolve the future problems of a modern metropolis.
Munich as arts centre, Munich as museum, Munich as Oktoberfest—the
stereotypic images come thick and fast. But how can more housing
be created; how can soaring rents be brought down to earth? What

about the mountains of rubbish? Which is more important, private or public transport? Multicultural open city, or closed Bavario-German sector—what *is* Munich, finally?

It's hard to avoid the thought that Munich is basking so obliviously in its rosy, progressive image that it doesn't take note of the potential time bombs on the horizon, even in an era in which the mighty cities of old—Vienna, Budapest, Prague and Berlin—are flowering again as serious competition.

Perhaps television is to blame, showing detective series set in a stage Munich which many city residents probably can't separate from the reality. Around 75,000 people are employed by the media here, so what's more natural than to use Munich as a set whenever one is needed? A constant stream of new, colourful images, a sugary icing for fast consumption, almost entirely effacing the texture of the old—the real?—Munich: what could be more palatable?

Maybe Munich-dwellers recognize themselves after the TV has been turned off and they look into the mirror. But in two out of three cases what they see in the mirror isn't the face of a born-and-bred Munichean, but that of a 'blow-in'. No wonder the city's statisticians have dropped the category of 'Munich-born'.

In fact, in Bavaria's 'metropolis with heart' (one of the more unspeakable images), the 'Prussians' (North Germans) are in the majority. But image wins out; Munich is Bavarian. The 'blow-ins' make visibly clumsy efforts to adapt, adopting the Loden uniform. At the turn of the century things were different. Schwabing denizens

Ludwigstraße and the Siegestor

then pointed out with pride the stand they were taking against the "dead-brained and beer-ied" natives (as the novelist Theodor Fontane described them).

Speaking of Schwabing, once the proud standard-bearer of free-thinking, rebellious, artistic Munich—whatever happened to you? People love to paint a picture of the avant-garde and biting intellectuals who once moved in your world of salons and studios. Now your streets are lined with pizza joints and bars, your boutiques and antique shops are run by wives in therapy, your old apartments and studios resound with dentists drilling, lawyers advising or Boards of Directors discussing art in progress: 'Concrete. It's what you make of it that counts.' What an image! It's been over 60 years, but tourists are still searching the streets like archaeologists, only to drown their disappointment in lukewarm cappuccinos on Leopold-straße.

Well, let's leave it at this. Munich is an image, an accepted myth, that effortlessly suppresses reality or, as Thomas Wolfe put it, '…in an astonishing way, the city is a great Germanic dream translated into life.'

Committed to (No-risk) Culture

Munich is proud of being one of the world's great cities, even if it is a bit on the small side for a major metropolis. (We may not be able to do everything Paris can, but we just love basking in the glory of great opera stars, lavish playhouses and glittering parties, whatever the cost.)

Take Gasteig, our cultural centre. This fortress-of-the-arts looming down from Rosenheimer Berg escaped financial ruin by a hair's breadth, and doesn't really look like the kind of concert hall where a Mozart could maintain his allegretto. Yet visitors have given the place a resounding vote of confidence, and thus the Philharmonic has quickly found acceptance, as have the library and the Adult Education Centre. (Now hefty entrance prices are extracted for concerts by artists from all over the world.)

Our commitment to culture is also demonstrated by gorgeous theatres: the Nationaltheater (our Opera House), the rococo jewel of the Cuvilliestheater, and the newly refurbished Prinzregententheater in Bogenhausen. Here you can trot out your dinner jacket and evening dress; here you'll be served 'culture' on a silver salver. Tickets can be got either by patience or through connections, ie hotel porters. But our theatres are better known for their 'safe-side' productions; new or challenging ideas are not exactly Munich's forte. Well known, light or classical plays are what's popular. Only a few small theatres, the Sword of Damocles of public subsidy constantly hanging over them, risk experiments behind the scenes of public interest.

On the other hand, the Deutsches Museum enjoys immense popularity, as does Gärtnerplatz, a lovely theatre extensively renovated in 1990 and devoted to the lighter Muses. These amusements have also cost the city dear.

More? Certainly! One of the largest libraries in Germany, the Staatsbibliothek (State Library) on Ludwigstraße; art galleries down Maximilianstraße and in Schwabing, the Old and New Pinakotheken, Glyptothek, Schack Gallery…

Lion Feuchtwanger once said that culture in the city is 'sated and fat'—but, unfortunately, 'timid and provincial' also apply. This theme has spawned a thousand arguments and complaints from reviewers and committees, politicians and cultural officers. The image question again.

The Philharmonic at the Gasteig

Munich Politics: Sofas, Reds, Greens, David and Goliath

'The combined forces of the CSU (Christian Social Union; right-wing party) and the Sofa Alliance toppled the mayor's motion.'

What, I hear you ask, has a sofa got to do with politics, apart from being an ideal place to sit out one's problems? Well, until recently, this particular sofa was an eminently political one. Two members of the SPD (Social Democratic Party, left-wing) broke ranks and determined that in future they would answer only to their own consciences, which in most cases just happened to fall in with the policies of the CSU. This left Mayor Kronawitter lacking majority support, but the situation was no threat to his staying in office—they're all old buddies down at the Munich Town Hall. When the Greens came along in 1984, it seemed at first that we were in for the spectre of Red-Green pandemonium, but the Greens soon ended up supplying the Head of the Department of the Environment—elected with the votes of the CSU.

In the latest election the Greens and the Social Democrats succeeded in gaining seats, only to be met with competition in the shape of yet another ecological grouping: the citizens' initiative 'David versus Goliath' (DaGG). At the same time, the CSU was likewise under fire from the extreme right-wing Republican Party.

But there was a surprise in store. 'Georgie' Kronawitter was elected by an overwhelming majority and, overnight, without batting an eyelid, unveiled a Red-Green coalition which completely overturned the political positions of the previous six years and sent Zöller, the ambitious CSU man and erstwhile secret ruler of the city in conjunction with the Sofa Alliance, into political retirement.

Meanwhile, the city's most pressing problems still await solutions—the housing shortage for example. The astronomical rents, unaffordable for one third of Munich's population—DM25 per square metre is no longer regarded as profiteering, but as the norm—are still seen as ineluctable fate. Other problems Munich is faced with are a dismal standard in refuse collection, a crisis at the under-staffed hospitals and an old sewerage system which is in urgent need of repair. The public transport system is in financial crisis and there is little money left to pay for the surrounding areas of Munich. The resources being allocated to the new republics of the former GDR have resulted in the depleting of Munich's communal budgets.

Local politics, in Munich as elsewhere, is a drama which can seldom boast of playing to packed houses. Thus nobody notices that in this 'mega-village' politics runs more along the lines of a Moreton-in-Marsh or a Gopher Prairie than of an international metropolis. Still, who cares? We're proud of the human factor in our politics! After all, where else would you find a political alliance with its very own sofa?

THE WOLPERTINGER

A stranger once came to Munich and met a native who told him the story of the Wolpertinger. The local wound up his account of this rare, indigenous creature with this coda: 'The Wolpertinger is a crazy animal.'

Few facts are certain, but we can confidently assure you that experts agree on the following points: the Wolpertinger is nocturnal, with rather poor vision in pitch-darkness, especially in frosty weather. Rare sightings indicate the creature shares certain physical attributes with a variety of other small animals, including the duck-billed platypus.

Visitors to Munich will almost certainly *not* be granted a glimpse of this shy animal, a pity since the legends surrounding the primordial beast could throw some light on some of the natives' own behaviour.

The Wolpertinger is famous not least of all for its striking physical appearance, a phenomenon which can inspire in newcomers in particular a state of *Obsessio Bavariae* (an important chapter heading in that definitive work, *Living with the Wolpertinger)* if they brood on the subject for too long.

In *Föhn* weather, a state of constant hallucination is the norm. Many people claim the Wolpertinger is furless, a fact that has moved sympathetic Municheans to fling off their clothes in the English Garden. But before we begin to speculate, let visitors proceed to the Hunting and Fishing Museum (Jagdmuseum) to admire the beast—stuffed. Maybe that'll put them in the picture.

On day one, new arrivals will be eager to see at first-hand all the sights they've heard so much about, to measure their images of Munich against the reality. In order not to court disappointment, to avoid risks and to spend the day where Munich's heart beats fastest, follow my itineraries as detailed below.

A Breath of Munich Air

A walk through the old town which takes in the most important sights; then, at day's end, a stroll through Schwabing.

—u4/5 and 3/6 to Odeonsplatz. Taxi to 'Odeonsplatz'—

Dallmayr, Beck, Hugendubel, Kaufhof . . . sorry, what I meant to say was Residence, Marienplatz, Town Hall, Old St Peter's, Viktualienmarkt! Let's start from the beginning. Come up out of the underground from **Odeonsplatz**, and the wide open spaces spread out before you—the wide boulevard of Ludwigstraße, straight as a die, with the Siegestor hazy in the distance, the Bavarian Arc de Triomphe. Turn around and the **Feldherrnhalle** confronts you, famous among other reasons as the site of Hitler's attempted putsch of 1923. It was in Munich that Hitler rose from being an ordinary member to leader of the NSDAP. On 8 November 1923, he believed himself strong enough to call for the fall of the Bavarian and national government. His attempted coup failed, and his demonstration was broken up here at the Feldherrnhalle, where 16 people

24

met their deaths. The Feldherrenhalle, completed in 1844 by Friedrich von Gartner, imitating the Loggia dei Lanzi in Florence, is otherwise a monument of praise to Bavarian military glory. It's attractive, with its lions like cuddly toys, and you'll find it hard to resist stroking their stone pelts.

Café am Hofgarten (Café Annast Bistro) is ideal for breakfast in the fresh air (from 9.15am). The colossal 17th-century **Theatinerkirche** opposite—with its magnificent altar and the graves of a Wittelsbach or two—stands bright ochre against the blue sky, its high dome some 71m (236ft) above the pavement. Sit in the sun and drink in the sight for a while, and then have a look at the Hofgarten.

Back at the Odeonsplatz, go left from the Feldherrenhalle into **Residenzstraße**. Historical house fronts and expensive shopping arcades are the main features, the Viscardigasse, on the right, leading to elegant Theatinerstraße. (During the Nazi period, some Municheans

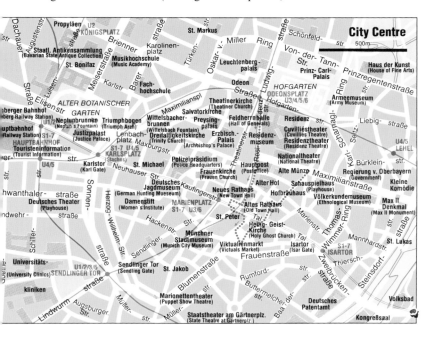

The Theatinerkirch

used to sneak down here to avoid the obligatory salute to the Nazi guard of honour at the Feldherrenhalle, and the alley got the name *Drückebergergasse*, or Cowards' Alley.)

The lovely Florentine Renaissance façade on the left may tempt art fans to a tour of the Antiquarium, porcelain collection, Cuvilliestheater and some of the State Chambers. The main entrance of the **Residenz** on Max-Joseph-Platz leads to the Schatzkammer (Treasury), where guided tours begin (Wednesday, 10am; Tuesday, Friday, 2pm; Saturday 2pm; Sunday, 11am, closed 1st Sunday of the month; DM6). Or you can examine all the objects of everyday use collected by kings and princes in the Treasury and the Residence Museum on your own: crowns, sceptres, orbs and so forth. Go straight on, at Max-Joseph-Platz, past the main Post Office with its columns, to **Marienhof**, formerly abused as a car park and now a green awaiting the construction of a pyramid of glass costing DM60 million.

The shops on the left in Dienerstraße are more interesting. **Dallmayr's** window displays are highly innovative, something which isn't actually necessary. Customers—upper-class and upper-class has-beens—will queue at the counters of the traditional delicatessen just to get a bag bearing the shop's name.

Finally, there's **Marienplatz**, where American and Japanese tongues alike wrap themselves reverently round *Gllakkenspiill* or *Grrrokkenspia*. With the thousands of others, throw back your heads and stare, fascinated, at the Gothic wedding cake façade of the New

Town Hall. And lo! High up in the tower, hardly visible, a few figures mechanically begin the Coopers' Dance, marking the end of the Plague (at 11am; in summer also at noon and 5pm).

Marienplatz is a place to see and be seen: tourists size up natives and natives eyeball tourists. A *Prinzregententorte* at the **Café Glockenspiel** (lift to the fourth floor, corner of Rosenstraße) will give you a new perspective on it all. If you yearn for higher things, climbing the tower of **Alter Peter** (Old St Peter's) on Rindermarkt will give you a view of the whole town. The ancient, creaking staircase will take you up to a height from which you can see as far as the Alps on a clear, *Föhn*-weather day. Those who don't dodge the stair-climbing are now ready for the **Viktualienmarkt**.

Interspersed throughout the colourful, bustling fruit, vegetable, cheese and sausage stalls, there are still a few genuine—or dressed-up—natives to be found who insist on regarding the Viktualienmarkt as their established territory. It's time to have a snack in the beer garden under the maypole: *weißwürscht* of course, white sausages, that abstruse delicacy which 'may not hear the noon bells' and which Prussians can only force down once a year at most. Accompaniments? *Brez'n,* salty bread twists, sweet mustard and a beer, naturally! By the way, the **Valentinsstüberl** on Dreifältigkeitsplatz or the inn, **Am alten Markt,** supply a roofed-over version of the same ultra-Bavarian ambience, complete with rustic décor.

Leave the Viktualienmarkt via Heiliggeiststraße, cross Tal and go past the **Weißes Bräuhaus,** down Maderbräustraße to Ledererstraße. A right then a left turn and you're in Orlandostraße, which ends at Platzl and the worldwide symbol of Munich and beer-drinking, the temple of the **Hofbräuhaus**. Even in the afternoon (although the evening is naturally more interesting, when thirsty representatives of many nations—plus the occasional native—worship at the Stein Shrine) you mustn't miss a look into this mighty building to sample the atmosphere.

The Kosttor leads you onto **Maximilianstraße**, where the scene changes dramatically to one of elegance and luxury. The **Hotel Vier Jahreszeiten,** opposite, is probably the best hotel in town, rubbing shoulders with successful galleries, really pricey shops etc. After a

At the Viktualienmarkt

short shopping tour, a taxi from outside the hotel or Max-Joseph-Platz will bring exhausted first-dayers back to base, perhaps after a drink at **Roma** (corner Franz-Josef-Strauß-Ring).

On the cards for the evening is a short stroll down **Leopoldstraße**, beginning at Siegestor and proceeding out of town on the right-hand side of the street. In summer there's a sort of arts and crafts market here, where hippies on the way from Ibiza to India used to sell what they'd been making in spring. As far as the products of today go, words fail. Opposite Ohmstraße, you could sip an aperitif in the VIPs' **Café Extrablatt**—unless you're already a VIP but would rather forget it.

Back on the other side of the street now, the most important question of the evening demands attention: where to eat? The fittest among you should refer to the evening tour of Schwabing (Tour 15) from now on. For the rest, here are a few places on either side of Leopoldstraße (booking recommended in some cases):

The Kaisergarten, at 34 Kaiserstraße (Tel: 347752), has a nice little beer garden. **Leopold**, at 50 Leopoldstraße, serves Bavarian fare. **Italy**, at 108 Leopoldstraße (Tel: 346403), features Italian cuisine. **Werneckhof**, at 11 Werneckstraße (Tel: 399936), specialises in French food. **Princess Garden**, at 25 Leopoldstraße (Tel: 343837), is great for Chinese, and **Noor Jahan**, at 5 Kaiserstraße (Tel: 348009), is one of Munich's best Indian restaurants.

Having catered for your physical wellbeing (you may also consult the *Dining Experiences* section towards the end of this guide for a complete listing of restaurants), and if you don't mind crowds of people pushing along the pavements until the wee hours, you might try to find a seat at one of the street cafés—**Roxy**, say. If you do manage to get a cappuccino in the end, you can think back over your first day in Munich, deliberately planned around the commonplace aspects of the city, and rest assured: there's more to Munich than clichés, as you'll soon see.

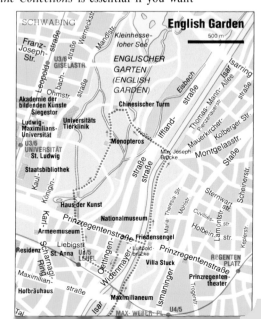

The Deutsches Museum and the River Isar

Visit to the Deutsches Museum; walk up the Isar; English Garden with Chinese Tower beer garden.

—s-Bahn Isartor or Tram 18 to Deutsches Museum. Taxi to 'Deutsches Museum, Haupteingang' (Main Entrance)—

Breakfast (from 8am) at **Café Schwabing** at Kurfürstenplatz. From here it's a pleasant 20-minute ride in the No. 18 tram along Barer Straße, past Stachus and Müller/Rumfordstraße to the Deutsches Museum. You can almost always find a taxi at Kurfürstenplatz.

On an island in the river, five minutes from Isartor, stands an imposing, large grey building exuding an air of tranquillity. Inside, a unique journey through the history and development of civilisation and technology awaits you. All you need is time, for there are people who have spent whole weeks in the **Deutsches Museum**!

Here you can get a miner's eye view of mines, inspect model bridges, tunnels or railway routes, try your hand at chemical and physical experiments. Here you'll see the first cars and aeroplanes, and under the roof in the Planetarium you'll be captivated by the night sky! More than 16,000 exhibits are displayed over five hectares, about ten acres. The *Guide to the Collections* is essential if you want to keep track of things. One thing you must do is be selective: don't be led astray by all the different rooms and possibilities. However, once you've submerged yourself in this new and old world of familiar but amazing things, you won't want to emerge when the museum finally closes at 5pm.

On the other hand, if you do find that after three hours signs of exhaustion and hunger-pangs are setting in, cross Boschbrücke Bridge and turn left into Erhardtstraße, where those with expensive tastes will want to try the restaurant in the European Patent Office, **Le Fleuron de l'Isar** (Monday–Friday only; 11am–2.30pm). **Asia**, on the corner of Corneliusstraße, offers set Chinese lunches at reasonable prices, and at **Il Cappuccino**, straight ahead in Kohlstraße, you can order a pizza or a plate of pasta. On the right of Ludwigsbrücke, on Rosenheimer Berg next to the monolithic Cultural Centre, **Il Museo**—recommended—has an attractive patio.

From Ludwigsbrücke—opposite the Deutsches Museum Congress Hall—continue along the Isar Canal and over the weir to the Praterinsel island. On the way, keep an eye out for **Father Rhine**, one of the loveliest fountains in Munich. On the gravel bank below the weir you may see a few nude sunbathers. (The nudity craze that spread through Munich at the start of the 1980s is still going strong.) On the right is that monument to art nouveau, the Müllersches Volksbad (Public Baths), where you can recover from

On the Ludwigsbrücke

your visit to the museum in marble baths under the sweep of a beautiful domed ceiling.

The **Praterinsel** begins at the Kabelsteg footbridge. Up to now it's been a peaceful spot, the home of the Alpenverein (Alpine Association) with its museum, and the schnapps distiller Riemenschneider. However, since Riemenschneider recently moved out, speculation has been rife. 'Dutch companies' wanted to build a 'gigantic' hotel complex on the island, but were stopped by the personal intervention of Munich's mayor. Although a photographer and an Indian textile designer have taken advantage of the situation and immediately moved into the buildings to turn them into an arts centre, it remains unclear as to what will happen to

this beautiful island. A multitude of art groups, theatre, dance and film projects would dearly love to find space in which to pursue their aims, but the Praterinsel remains unused.

From the Steg footbridge, past the children's playground—always popular—cross another bridge over the Auer Mühlbach stream, then continue up the left bank of the river for a while. Pass under Maximiliansbrücke, where the ground slopes steeply down again. Up at the top of the slope is the magnificent **Maximilianeum**, seat of the Bavarian State Parliament (Landtag) since 1949. An urban paradise unfolds on the other side of the bridge: wide footpaths and meadows beckon, for lazing around, playing badminton or stealing 4forty winks on a bench. Down river the newly regilded figure of the **Friedensengel** (Angel of Peace) glistens above the tree tops.

At Luitpoldbrücke Bridge you can make a detour to St-Anna-Platz in the Lehel district, and head towards the English Garden from there instead of following the Isar up to Tivolibrücke. If the present idyll suffices, stay on the Isar. This part of the bank up to Tivolibrücke looks just like the foothills of the Alps. The tower of the **Bogenhausener Kirchlein** (little church) peeps over invitingly. Liesl Karlstadt the comedienne, Erich Kästner and Rainer Werner Fassbinder are all buried in its rural churchyard. Another ten minutes and over Tivolibrücke will bring you to the Chinese Tower.

If you decide on the alternate route, cross the Isar by Luitpoldbrücke and turn left off Prinzregentenstraße into Reitmorstraße, and right from Robert-Koch-Straße to the looming towers of **Annakirche** (St Anne's Church). This baroque façade, at first sight rather unprepossessing, conceals a jewel well worth the effort of discovering: a beautiful monastic church by the Brothers Asam. Triftstraße and Wagmüllerstraße will return you to Prinzregentenstraße, where you enter the English Garden.

Here, where the wild stream of the Eisbach roars along, a broad meadow unrolls before you. Proceed to the right and follow the main path past **Monopteros**, a small folly on the hill to the left,

The Chinese Tower

straight to the **Chinese Tower**. A hum of voices fills the air; beer steins clink at the counters; the scent of sausages and *sauerkraut* wafts over. Under the wooden pagoda roof, in a hubbub of screaming children and barking dogs, oompah music and Argentinian guitars, is where Munich meets Munich; glamour girls and VIPs, the homeless and castle owners, Bavarians and Prussians, black and white, pink, lilac, brown, green, yellow—all are united in hoisting huge beer steins. So, join them, sit down and enjoy the view, as (almost) all of the glittering rainbow of Munich parades before your eyes! Then, you'll emulate Ludwig Thoma's Munich porter Aloysius (from his tale, *A Munich Man In Heaven*), ordering 'a beer, another beer, and another beer,' until finally, like Aloysius, you really need 'divine counsel' to find your way out of the garden in the dark. (Munich beer gardens close at 11pm.) If a 15-minute walk is still within your capabilities, try to get to Giselastraße. At this time of night there are still plenty of pedestrians only too happy to point out the way. From there, go to the U3/6 station on Leopoldstraße. Otherwise, you can try to hail a taxi on Tivolibrücke or take the No. 20 tram back into town.

Day 3

The Changing Face of Munich

An exploration of Haidhausen, a prime example of the transformation of an old quarter into a 'metropolitan district'.

—Tram 18 to Deutsches Museum. Taxi to 'Gasteig'—

Haidhausen, older than Munich, was once an old, established traditional quarter in its own right. Then it was forgotten and allowed to go to seed. Where once the brick makers, labourers, carters and coffin makers had to live, old people subsequently found solace in the district's lower rents, students were happy with the less than luxurious conditions and foreigners brought new life to the streets and squares. There were once little corner shops, carpenters' workshops in back yards and the pub where locals got drunk at weekends.

But times change. Many of the old houses have been demolished, and 'high-value urban infrastructure' has taken over Rosenheimer Berg in the wake of the monolithic Gasteig Cultural Centre. Even the Bürgerbräukeller had to go, that place, redolent with symbolism,

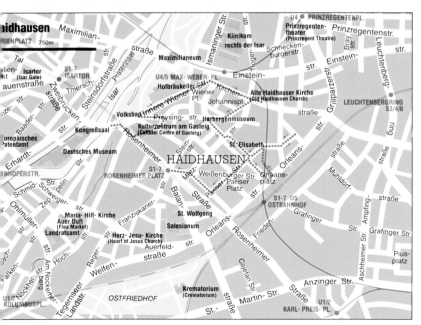

The Gasteig Cultural Centre

where Hitler made his first public appearances and narrowly escaped death when Eisner, the Swiss carpenter attempted to assassinate him in 1939. From Rosenheimer Berg, the new avatars of the fast buck—computers, the media and art-as-a-commodity—advance inexorably along the old streets. The corner pub is now called 'Hemingway's Bar', and futons fill the window of the old greengrocer's.

Let's begin where the changes are at their most obvious, at **Gasteig**. From Lüdwigsbrücke Bridge the new brick cultural centre looks like a lumpy battleship. The Philharmonic, Germany's most popular library and the Adult Education Centre (Volkshochschule) have found a home here and regularly arrange exhibitions. The building was quickly accepted and, once inside, it's possible to forget the shortcomings of the exterior architecture.

Leave the palace of culture by the rear exit (Kellerstraße) and, before you do anything else, have breakfast in (contrasting) style. Gasteig Cafeteria is no place to linger; but **Café Stöpsel** (Holzhofstraße and left to **Preysingplatz**) is where alternative spirits hold court in the shadow of the church. It's an idyllic spot, especially if the weather permits sitting outside.

Down Preysing/Stubenvollstraße, towards town, is another idyll on **Innere Wiener Straße** (on the right heading away from town):

The changing face of Haidhausen

the Loretto Chapel. Right next to it is another focus for architectural rapacity: the former premises of the Hofbräuhaus brewery.

A shift of production to the east of town and an extensive fire in 1987—nicely timed, say some—'produced' a site in a prime location on the banks of the Isar. Those much-vaunted architectural competitions have already taken place. What is supposed to be preserved is the **Kellergarten** (one of the loveliest beer gardens in Munich) and the Hofbräukeller restaurant, both directly on **Wiener Platz**. Here, too, old 'lodgings' typical of Haidhausen have been renovated and lend the square a village atmosphere, compounded by the kiosks, market stalls and food stands.

The other side of the district's sociological character swigs cappuccino at **Café Wiener Platz**, owned by actress Iris Berben. My favourite spot in Haidhausen is **Johannisplatz** (right from Kirchenstraße), with its neo-Gothic church towers like newly sharpened pen-

Johannisplatz

cils. Here the old houses still stand, old people still sit under shady trees, children still play. The charm of this square, screened from the bustle of commerce, never fails to catch me by surprise, as if it belonged to another era. Perhaps that's why the outwardly unprepossessing **Johannis-Café** has survived (open 11am–1pm, Saturdays till 3am), wherein the ageing suburban gigolo meets up with the local butcher, and punks rub shoulders with yuppies.

Follow Kirchenstraße and take a look at the lives of 'little men' and the history of the district at No. 24, the attractive **Haidhausen Museum** (Monday–Wednesday, 4–6pm; Tel: 4485292). Kirchenstraße has managed to preserve its pre-war character as far as Seeriederstraße, but at the junction the low rent council housing so much in evidence brings us back to the 1990s. The old **Haidhausen Church** and graveyard a little way up the hill allows the idyll a lease on life.

From this detour you turn left into **Wolfgangstraße** where, after passing the **Blauer Engel** (see Tour 16: *Going Out in Haidhausen),*

Alternative culture lives on

we come across the **Kriechbaumhof**, newly built and with a slightly out-of-place air; hardly in a position to conjure up the atmosphere of the old 'lodgings district'.

Follow Preysingstraße and turn left into **Wörthstraße**, where **Café Voila** affords you a good place to rest and recuperate. Your exploration continues at **Bordeauxplatz**, where the so-called French Quarter begins. The street names—such as Sedan, Metz, Paris, etc—all hark back to the Franco-German War of 1870–1. (Led by General von Moltke, the superior German troops triumphed at Sedan on 1 September 1870, and Napoleon was captured. German troops marched into Paris and France was forced to accept a bitter peace settlement.)

This part of Haidhausen was built during Germany's 'Industrial Revolution' *(Gründerzeit),* when a wave of speculation washed over the area. Tenements were built to house the masses of casual labourers, and they still form the basis of the housing here today.

At **Orleansplatz**, the years spent rebuilding the Ostbahnhof haven't succeeded in removing the barrenness, so turn straight off

to the left down **Belfortstraße**, unless you want to end your expedition here and take advantage of Ostbahnhof's range of public transport.

In this part of Haidhausen apartments are still rented, not owned outright. Little stores, galleries, studios, health food shops and back yard cafés all give the area the flair of a Latin Quarter. Make a detour to the right down **Breisacher Straße** and walk back along the other side of the street to Pariser Platz, crossing Wörthstraße on the way. The myriad small shops here, often with unusual and/or artistically alternative wares, can surprise browsers with curios

The Kriechbaumhof

which are seldom to be found anywhere else in the city. Following **Pariser Straße**, then turning to the left into Lothringer Straße down to Weißenburger Platz, take the opportunity to lay in supplies of tea (in **Teeladen**) and more.

At **Rosenheimer Platz** at the very latest, deal with the question of what to do with the rest of the afternoon. No two ways about it— go to the **Kellergarten** of the Hofbräuhaus on Wiener Platz! In fact, since it's my favourite beer garden, I'm probably sitting not far away from you. From here, you can proceed with the evening programme without a break. But if you want to come back later, please, for the sake of the residents, use public transport (U4/5, Tram 18 to Max-Weber-Platz, S-Bahn to Rosenheimer Platz) or taxi. There are no parking spaces, and anyone parking on the pavement is liable to have his tyres 'ventilated'.

The following half-day programmes cover either an interesting aspect of the city or a specific theme. Choose whatever interests you most—and off you go.

Munich Explored

1. Art and Intellect

A stroll through the Museum and University District.

—U2 to Königsplatz. Taxi 'Königsplatz'—

This morning programme begins at Königsplatz, where Ludwig I transformed his dream of creating an 'Athens on the Isar' into reality. On each side of the **Propylaea**, the **Antikensammlung (Collection of Antiquities)** and the **Glyptothek**, built in the Classicist style and modelled on Athenian architecture, house probably the most significant collections of classical sculpture in Germany.

Breakfast in the **Café in der Glyptothek** (open daily 10am–4pm, except Thursday noon-4pm) provides an Olympic start to the day and is the ideal prelude to visiting the Glyptothek. The **Königsplatz** area still bears the scars of its National Socialist past. Hitler had the square paved with granite for his rallies (this reminder of the past was recently eradicated by planting grass). But if you leave the square by **Brienner Straße** and go towards Karolinenplatz, you will see the plinths of the Nazi 'Temple of Honour' at the junction of Arcisstraße and Meiserstraße where the SS once stood guard; blown up after the war, it now lies in ruins and is covered in undergrowth.

The obelisk at **Karolinenplatz** is a monument to the 30,000 Bavarian soldiers who lost their lives in Napoleon's march on Moscow. House No. 5 once belonged to the Bruckmanns, the publishing family who gave Hitler considerable support and served as his introduction into Munich business circles.

Ten minutes' walk down **Barer Straße** brings you to two further highlights of the Munich museum scene, the **Old and New Pinakotheken**. Anyone unable to resist these can spend the rest of the day here. On the right in the car park there's usually a circus tent advertising a slightly more ephemeral form of cultural activity, and sometimes you'll find a touring theatre group here and other 'strolling players'. Whenever I'm in this area I take the opportunity to drop into the Far Eastern shop in **Gabelsbergerstraße**.

If you cross the park between the two Pinakotheken, you come to **Arcisstraße**, parallel to Barer Straße. Follow this road and you'll find an oasis of man-made charm, the **Old North Cemetery (Alter Nördlicher Friedhof)**. Here life and death have managed to arrange an improbable modus vivendi: in the summer, students from the Technical University bask in the sun between the gravestones, children playing football use the crosses as goal posts, building site workers eat their sandwiches, yuppies jog to and fro, and old people pass the time in conversation. Leave the cemetery by the Arcisstraße exit, go down Schnorrstraße to Schraudolphstraße and turn right into **Schellingstraße**.

The **Osteria Italiana** on the corner used to be called **Osteria Bavaria** in the 1920s and was Hitler's local. Nowadays it's a popular restaurant with the film and media crowd. On the corner of Barer and Schellingstraße, a colourful cross-section of people while away their time playing pool or cards in the **Schelling-Salon,** a pub rich in tradition which still carries a lingering trace of Bohemianism in its smoke filled air.

Next, turn left into **Türken-straße**, where boutiques,

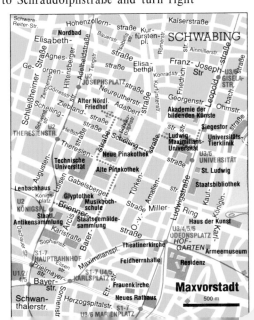

The covered courtyard, University

shops full of knick-knacks and casual clothes stores are the main features, but there are still a few establishments in this area which you might make a note of for later on: **Alter Simpl** and **Charivari** (both open till 3am, or 4am on Saturday, closed Sunday). **Simpl**, with its long history—Ringelnatz and Heine are obligatory inclusions in its list of regulars—still seems to be a landing place for famous faces and, after 1am, **Charivari** fills up with a murky mixture of urbanites, sometimes terribly artistic, sometimes simply terrible.

Café undsoweiter or **Adria** the ice cream parlour will supply you with a cappuccino before you have a look in the **Zweitausendeins** bookshop just before Blütenstraße. In the **Amalienpassage** (behind 84 Türkenstraße) you may explore the possibilities of **Café Oase**, or mingle with the Italo-Bavarian jetset at **Rosario's**—that is, as long as Rosario doesn't mind. (Only recognizable celebrities and their 'mates' get served.) Amalienpassage, which will probably appear in sociological treatises of the future as 'Munich's first Be-there-or-be-square' venue, emerges in **Amalienstraße**. A journey through the scene of many a student's humiliation, the university just opposite, is the next item on the programme. (Even when I was a student, I never felt comfortable in the place.) In the **covered courtyard** (right from the entrance, up a few steps, then left) there is a memorial plaque to the Scholls and the resistance movement known as the White Rose—a few courageous souls who unswervingly gave their all for freedom and democracy while Munich preened itself on being the capital of the Nazi movement. Ludwig Maximilian University was transferred from Landshut to Munich by King Ludwig I in 1826; its magnificent and impressive buildings were designed by Friedrich von Gärtner. Back in the sunshine on Geschwister-Scholl-Platz, now is a good time to head off to the left and look at the **Siegestor** (Victory Arch), without which no collection of Munich snapshots would be complete.

2. Munich's Green Belt

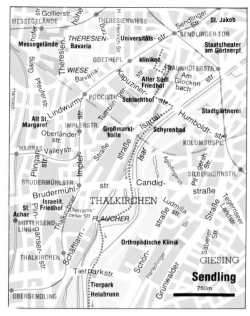

A walk outside the city, along the southern part of the River Isar, the Flaucher beer garden, Flaucher footbridge (Flauchersteg), the delights of swimming in the Isar, Hellabrunn Zoo.

—U3/6 to Goetheplatz. Taxi 'Rothmundstraße'—

Here's one of the reasons why people find it so hard to tear themselves away from Munich; the River Isar to the south of **Wittelsbacher Bridge** has everything that the 1970s regarded as the epitome of 'quality of life'. Those bent on marketing the city call this 'high leisure value'. Straight after leaving the 'big city' you're plunged into a completely different town with an atmosphere of small time respectability, an echo of childhood. Where else would you be able to jump into a river in the buff, only a stone's throw from a teeming metropolis, without being locked up or poisoned?

This morning (or afternoon) could easily stretch into a whole day. So, if you anticipate being overtaken by spontaneous desires, remember to take a swimming costume with you—even if you turn out not to need it in most places—plus a towel to lie on, suntan oil and perhaps a sweater for the evening chill.

Rothmund is a possibility for breakfast in the area (Rothmundstraße/corner Maistraße, Monday–Friday, open from 9am; Saturday/Sunday, from 10.30am).

Walking through the **Old South Cemetery (Alter Südfriedhof)** to Baldeplatz afterwards (Maistraße, Waltherstraße, left into Thalkirchnerstraße and through the side entrance of the cemetery; proceed to the right), will give you a chance to get acquainted with a whole troupe of Munich's illustrious sons and daughters, from Spitzweg the painter to Fraunhofer the inventor to the explorer of Japan, who had his gravestone made in the form of a Buddhist stupa. Cross

Kapuzinerstraße, turn left and you'll be on **Baldeplatz** in five minutes. Follow the Isar upstream, past the Rodenstock spectacle factory on the right after a handful of old houses, and bear left where Wittelsbacherstraße runs into Ehrengutstraße. After the Brau-nauer railway bridge, the metalled road ends at **Flaucher Park**. The trees rustle gently, the birds twitter, the Isar babbles along, and only the huge chimneys of the power station on the other side of the Isar Canal remind us that we're still in the city. The Middle Ring Road can be crossed safely via the subway at **Brudermühl Bridge**.

From here on, Flaucher Park is pure paradise, opening out into an expanse of grass where the youth of today is still flying the flag of fitness, just as we used to do on Sunday mornings. Joggers, cyclists, mothers, prams, tricycles, every breed of dog conceivable, every possible variation on the theme of the human visage—all are out here devoting themselves, just as was intended, to the pursuit of leisure. At this time of the morning we pass the **Flaucher beer garden** with heavy hearts since, after all, we *have* only just had breakfast (we can always come back later), and follow the paved road to the beginning of the legendary Flauchersteg (Flaucher footbridge) on the left. Here you can buy provisions at the new kiosk to keep you going till the zoo.

Flauchersteg . . . well, what can I say? It's beyond my writing powers to adequately de-scribe the scene on summer days when, packed shoulder to shoulder along the gravel banks under the wooden footbridge, soaking up the sun, an amorphous mass of sizzling, naked flesh proves as keen to show itself off as are the passers-by to gape at it. In the evenings, however, countless barbecues are set up on the gravel banks of the river and sausages, spare ribs and more are grilled—one of summer's standard pleasures for Municheans.

The Flaucher Bridge leads to a footpath which will take you to **Thalkirchner Bridge**, where the grounds of Hellabrunn Zoo begin, a walk lasting around 10 minutes. But, if you've had enough, turn right over the bridge and after five minutes you'll come to the new U3 or to a taxi rank. If you're still thirsty for sunshine and aren't too keen on a trip to the zoo right now, continue down the path along the Isar to the **Marienklausenbrücke**.

Upstream from here are countless chances to experience the pleasures of swimming in Munich, both in bathing- and birthday-suit. You can get back into town via the 57 bus (taking you to the U3 head station) from the other side of the river beyond the landing stage at the campsite.

However, a visit to **Hellabrunn Zoo** (adults DM6, children DM3) is really a must, and you should allow yourself a few hours for it. The zoo was designed in 1928 and based on varied aspects of geography, so that a tour of the zoo will take you through all the various kinds of natural habitat. The guide book—recommended—costs DM3.

If the weather is hot and sunny, it's worth considering reversing the order of this tour and beginning with the zoo early in the morning (zoo opening times: April–September, 8am–6pm; October–March 9am–5pm) and then looking for a good spot on the river. As evening falls, you can make tracks for the Flaucher beer garden and head for a night on the tiles

in the Glockenbach district afterwards, via **Zoozie's** at Baldeplatz. Your only worry will be what to do with that wet towel!

3. The Upper Ten Thousand

A walk through Old Bogenhausen and Arabellapark.

—U4/5 to Max-Weber-Platz. Taxi 'Wiener Platz'—

One of the best and most venerable areas in Eastern Munich is **Bogenhausen**, where Victorian houses rub shoulders with art nouveau façades, luxury villas covered with ivy keep company with elegant apartment blocks and futuristic high-rise buildings stretch their slender necks.

After breakfast at the **Café Wiener Platz** (from 8am; subway to Max-Weber-Platz), take the subway one station further and get off at **Prinzregentenplatz**. You should be in the perfect mood to take in a few impressions of local housing styles (**Possartstraße** and Shakespeareplatz, then left into **Cuvilliesstraße** and along to **Ismaningerstraße**). But a closer look will enlighten you: no one lives here any more. Clinics, solicitors, company and music production offices as well as advertising agencies you will find. But it really seems to have become economically unviable to live in your

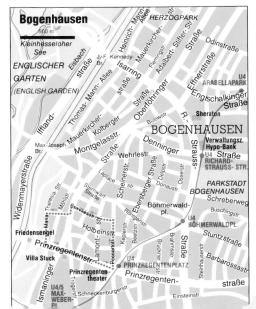

own house. It's a much better idea to invest the rent you take in, and leave: there are still a few nice places to go dotted around the globe. This situation becomes clear (go left into Ismaningerstraße, then right into Siebertstraße) in **Maria-Theresia-Straße**. When everyone leaves the office in the evening, the whole area is—to put it mildly—deserted.

Still, Bogenhausen has more to offer than just 'old houses'. Go left along Maria-Theresia-Straße and you'll see a reminder of the area's magnificence, the **Friedensengel** (Angel of Peace) on its column in Prinzregentenstraße. Two minutes' walk out of town, on the right at the corner of Ismaningerstraße, is the **Villa Stuck**, a palatial town house built between 1897 and 1914, the residence of Franz von Stuck, the 'painter prince', and the perfect symbol of parvenuism in art, ie anyone who still believes in art for art's sake has only himself to blame. The house now belongs to the city council and has housed some of the most interesting art exhibitions of the last 20 years.

The Chinese restaurant in the villa, **Taitung**, used to be one of the favourites of the Bavarian politician Franz-Josef Strauß. One block further up, however, there's a gourmets' paradise of rather a different stripe, festooned with garlands and twinkling with lights: **Käfer**. The ground floor houses a supermarket crammed with delicacies, and if your bill's high enough, the staff will carry your purchases out to your waiting Daimler. On the first floor there is a restaurant mentioned in gourmet guide books—just the thing for anyone dining out on a company account, or wanting to impress model girlfriends (booking recommended).

Continuing out of town along Prinzregentenstraße, usually choked with traffic, we find ourselves back where we started, at the **Prinzregententheater**. Since its restoration in 1988, this theatre has regained its old glory after many years of quiet disintegration. Quantities of private donations and the requisite public funds (the Germans say 'art is aptitude', which the inhabitants of Munich render as 'if you can do it, that's all there is to it.') enabled it to rise again like a phoenix from the ashes. The theatre is trying to create an identity for itself by staging striking productions. If you thirst for more modernity, Bogenhausen has something to offer you. Take the U4 (there are taxis at Prinzregentenplatz, too) to **Arabellapark**, only a stone's throw away: this area is Munich's Manhattan. You'll find real tower blocks here, the oldest skyscraper in Munich, the Arabella apartment block so beloved by potential suicides, the Sheraton Hotel (no further comment necessary), the faceless lump of the Ministry of the Environment and—the pinnacle of architectural triumph—the silhouette of the Hypobank's glass and aluminium towers, as fascinating a structure as it is controversial. No photographer can resist this subject, so be sure to take enough film. Arabellapark was the scene of a new chapter in Munich's architectural history. Forty years ago all this was still wasteland, until the 1980s saw the construction of a 'Neuperlach' for the upwardly mobile. Now, 50,000 people live here and there are several restaurants, bars, two out-of-the-ordinary cinemas, schools and shopping centres.

If you pause after this long morning to rest your weary feet in one of the cafés on **Rosenkavalierplatz** (**Föhn**, for instance, weekdays 10am–1am, weekends 7pm–1am), you'll be able to see the fashion plates swan past, and sense the pulsing life of this new town. However, if you yearn for the patina of age and a time when a home was something better than just a roof over your head for the few hours when the office is closed, then take the No. 154 bus from Arabellapark U-Bahn station down Montgelas Hill. If you get out at **Mauerkircher-straße**, you can follow the Isar from the Tivoli Bridge past houses it's truly a privilege to live in. When you come back along Pienzenauerstraße, you'll know why people love living in Munich.

A different perspective on the Hypobank

4. Shopping Fever

Shopping expedition from the Hauptbahnhof via Stachus and the pedestrian zone to Isartor.

—U1–5, S-Bahn to Hauptbahnhof. Taxi to 'Hauptbahnhof'—

Today, I mean business; it's shopping time. Shopping in Munich isn't always an unmitigated pleasure, after all. The enormous range of goods on offer gives you the constant feeling that you could have bought better (cheaper, more elegant etc) things elsewhere; that you've just bought the wrong thing (or something you didn't need); or that, actually, you really don't need anything at all. A word of warning: Munich shop assistants rival Parisians in their lack of helpfulness. So, before you plunge into the hurly-burly of the shops, you'd better remember to take your sense of humour with you. (Humour's when you laugh despite everything.)

High-tech and hi-fi fans will want to start at the **Station Concourse** with a small detour down **Schillerstraße** (don't worry, all those porn movies and rip-off bars are harmless), where they'll find everything their hearts desire, from cheapo computers to the highest of high-tech.

Other mortals are faced with an immediate choice between **Schützenstraße** and the **Hertie Building**. Schützenstraße is reserved for pedestrians and has no real shopping identity of its own, so it will probably be more interesting to wander through Hertie, the covered alternative. From the **Station Lower Level**, you can cut through the **Market Halls (Markthallen)** of Munich's delicatessen king Käfer; if you missed breakfast at the hotel, you can catch up at **Lenotre** with fresh croissants.

After you've checked out the various floors, end up in the basement in the store's food halls: it's hard to resist having elevenses here—pasta, gyros, fish, Bavarian specialities, vegetarian dishes, wine, champagne, coffee, beer and so on make up a real cornucopia.

From here you can pass without a break to the underground **Stachus shopping centre**. (Even the least brainy Prussian by now knows the story of where Stachus got its name but, just in case… Once upon a time, a certain Eustachius Föderl ran a beer garden here. Municheans have never been able to get on with its official name of **Karlsplatz**.) Stachus underground means clouds of pizza-, sausage- and U-Bahn-scented air wafting up to greet the explorer, milling crowds, fast food débris, glass fronted shops, naked consumerism, difficulties in orientation, etc, etc. Is this why the city of Munich decided to place its **Information Office** here? You run around in circles until you see a staircase up to Neuhauserstraße, where the Stachus fountain will refresh you and the **pedestrian zone** begins.

You have to see it to believe it. Where else can you see *pedestrian* jams during rush hour which are only just this side of stampedes? If you want to get through you need the nerves of a slalom champion to avoid falling headlong over the concrete flower tubs! But forget all that, we're here to shop! You can pay a visit to the Deutsche Bank (with cash machine), and get yourself DM400 which, if you're lucky, may last you until Marienplatz.

Behind **Karlstor**, built in 1315, you'll find an opulent perfumery in **Karstadt im Oberpollinger**. Before Kapellenstraße, you can take a look at the **Bürgersaal (Assembly Hall),** with its crypt-like subterranean vaults. Otherwise, it's just one shop after another and, at last, the **Augustiner Restaurant**, where you can allow yourself a break in the shell-domed hall. Then, you're off again: shops to the left of you, shops to the right of you. St Michael's Church is on the left as well; the **Beate Uhse** sex-shop on the right. (The Jesuit founders of St Michael's, that supreme symbol of the Counter-Reformation, would have enjoyed having such a neighbour.) Ludwig II is buried in the Princes' Crypt (Monday–Friday, 10am–1pm; 3–4.45pm; Saturday, 10am–3pm). The **Hunting and Fishing Museum (Jagd- und Fischereimuseum)** is on the corner of Augustinerstraße. If you're not interested in staring at the wall of video screens in front of **WOM** (Munich's largest record shop), go left down Augustinerstraße to the **Frauenkirche (Cathedral)** You certainly won't find a seat in **Bratwurst-Glöckl**, so con-

tinue down Sporenstraße to **Weinstraße**. Go right here and you're at the very heart of commerce—**Marienplatz**. Shops in this area have no need to worry about where their customers will come from: **Hugendubel** (the biggest bookshop in Munich), **Beck** (the apotheosis of neo-Bavarian upper-class consumerism) and, of course, **Kaufhof** (not for claustrophobes), will be only too happy to confirm this. We've missed the obligatory Glockenspiel (carillon) at 11am anyway (also at noon in summer). But you might consider paying a visit to the **Toy Museum (Spielzeugmuseum)** in the Old Town Hall—well worth a look. Even the Viktualienmarkt will have to do without you today. Go straight ahead down **Tal**. But after the Heiliggeistkirche church and the souvenir shop (opposite is a branch of the Sparkasse-Bank, with cash machine), your gaze drifts across the street to the **Weißes Bräuhaus**. And what a heavenly vision swims before your eyes: 'genuine, bloody-minded' Munich serving staff, Weißbier (that heavenly brew), roast pork and a good cross-section of people! Perhaps some other time? Or, how about right now, if you can find a place? No, your duty to spend calls. After all, Tal is the centre of the furnishing stores. At last, in the distance, **Isartor** indicates that your shopping binge is nearly over and invites harassed consumers into the **Valentin-Museum** (Monday, Tuesday, Saturday 11.01—yes, that's not a misprint—am–5.29pm; Sunday, 10.01am–5.29pm). See, if your sense of humour's still intact, there's still **The Isartor**   something to laugh about at the end of the consumer trail.

5. Royal Munich

Nymphenburg Palace: tour of the Palace grounds, Gallery of Beauties and Marstallmuseum (Royal Stables Museum).

—U1, 12 tram or 33 bus from Rotkreuzplatz.
Taxi to 'Platz der Freiheit'—

If you like, have breakfast today at a café which exerts itself to maintain an atmosphere of cool stylishness at all times: the **Café Freiheit** at **Platz der Freiheit**. Then it's off to Nymphenburg. It's a 20-minute walk down Frundsbergstraße/Ruffinistraße (**Ruffini**, on the corner of Orffstraße, is a breakfast alternative) to the start of the **Nymphenburg Canal**, in winter a skating and curling paradise for one and all. Another 20-minute stroll down the Southern Approach brings you to **Nymphenburg Palace**. If all this walking's too much for you, take the No. 12 tram from Rotkreuzplatz to the corner of Kanalstraße and Notburgastraße.

When you get to the roundel with the fountain, keep going north, where the **Nymphenburger Porcelain Manufactory** (Monday—Friday 8.30am–noon and 0.30–5pm) awaits your visit. However, the main attraction, for Municheans at least, is the **Palace Park**.

In 1664, when the Royal Elector, Ferdinand Maria, laid the foundation stone of his summer residence, the palace still lay a long way outside the city in idyllic countryside. Until well into the 1800s it was built up, extended and replanned until it had grown into a magnificent urban palace. At the main portal, a spacious, severely arranged classical garden in the French style spreads out before the visitor. But if you head off to the left, 'into the bushes', you'll see quite a different aspect of the park: here, it's a total wilderness, parts of it like a primeval jungle. And this is precisely why it's so popular, because you can be fooled into thinking the city is far, far away. There are also summer houses and temples hidden among the

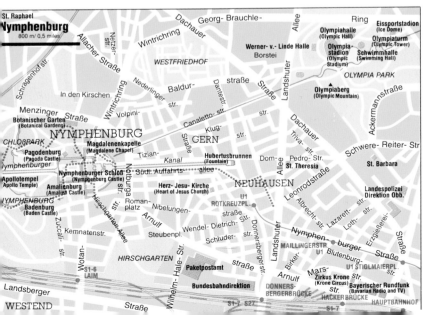

foliage. On the left-hand side of the park is **Amalienburg**, a gorgeous little rococo masterpiece; further towards the Large Lake (Großer See) is **Badenburg**, one of the few surviving bathing houses of the 18th century. Once round the lake, you can contemplate life in the peaceful **Apollotempel** or indulge in dreams of far off lands in the Chinese-style **Pagodenburg**. If you want, you can turn your tour of the park into a picnic or a romantic day with a book, and, at least for a while, forget the big city.

From the Pagodenburg, it's best to head back to the main canal, where you have a fine view of the whole park from the Cascades. And that's not all: in the **Botanical Garden** in the northern part of the park, hundreds of varieties of trees cast their shade and little

fountains babble softly between colourful beds of roses and tulips. The **Palmenhaus** is a particular attraction, with tropical and subtropical plants: sections of it are humid enough to make your glasses steam up, while the 'desert department' is so dry that visitors hurry gasping to the Palmengarten to gulp down cooling drinks. In the **Terrarium** next door, a few snakes and lizards doze quietly by themselves.

Back at the roundel, the best plan is to begin at the **Royal Stables Museum (Marstallmuseum)**. Here you'll find all the coaches, carriages and sleighs you usually see only in historical films. In the palace itself you can pay homage to the female face and form in Ludwig I's **Gallery of Beauties (Schönheitsgalerie)**. Thirty-seven beauties, to be precise, and their portraits are all here competing for the spectator's attention. Lola Montez is the most famous of these; her open affair with Ludwig turned into an affair of State in 1848. As you wander through this unusual collection, compare the beauties of Munich past with those you have seen in Munich present.

A good place to conduct contemporary research in this field is the restaurant **Zur Schwaige** in the left, or south, wing of the palace. Even better, follow Hirschgartenstraße behind Zur Schwaige, and you'll come to that most traditional of all the beer gardens, the **Hirschgarten**. There you can examine the faces and draw your own conclusions. From nearby Romanplatz you can return to town by tram, bus or taxi.

The Royal Stables Museum

6. Olympia

Tour of the BMW Museum with visit to the works; walk through the Olympic Park; visit to Papa Timofei.

—U2/3 to Olympiazentrum. Taxi to 'BMW Museum'—

You have to give the **Bavarian Motor Works** their due. Their contribution to Munich architecture, the main administration building in the form of the world's biggest four cylinder, is just as striking as the giant egg cup of the BMW **Museum** next door (9am–4pm, DM4.50). Inside the egg cup, the visitor climbs up a spiral staircase, reviewing the history of the automobile: from veteran chugalong to the state-of-the-art elegance. The designers of this exhibition have managed to illustrate the history of BMW with a wealth of historical material, creating a fascinating document of contemporary history.

If you want to delve deeper into the technical aspects of BMW, you can take a **guided tour of the production area** starting at the museum cash desk. Booking in advance might be a good idea, since the tours are extremely popular (Monday–Friday, 9am–1.30pm; 1–1.15 pm in English; bookings Tel: 38953639).

Across Georg-Bräuchle-Ring is the largest single-site sports complex in Europe. The **Olympic Park (Olympiagelände)** attained

worldwide fame for its unique roof (among other things) designed by Stuttgart architect Behnisch and composed of acrylic plates held together by a net of steel which arches over the sports grounds.

If you plan to turn up with a bag full of sports gear, your first chance to use it will be on the **Ice Rink (Eissporthalle**, 8.30am–noon; 1.30–5pm; 6.30–10pm), where you can also hire skates. Then it's out with the swimsuit and over to the swimming pool, not forgetting the **television tower (Fernsehturm)** in between, which is hard to overlook at 290 metres or 950 feet (9am–midnight; revolving restaurant, 11am–5.30pm; 6.30–11.45pm; Tel: 3081039). There's a great view of the city and the surrounding countryside as far as the Alps—especially in Föhn weather, with its clear blue skies—from the observation platform.

The **swimming pool** (Monday, 10am–10.30pm; Tuesdays, Thursdays 7am–6pm; other days, 7am–10.30pm) is 50m (55 yards) in length, has a separate diving pool, sauna and whirlpool and a lot more to offer than just a chance to crawl up and down the lanes. The **Olympiahalle** next door stages events ranging from handball games to pop concerts to carnival balls, and there are a restaurant and bowling alley too.

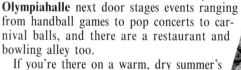

If you're there on a warm, dry summer's afternoon at the weekend, check out the free open air pop concerts at the **Theatron** behind the swimming pool.

If it's Saturday afternoon, Bavaria's First Division football team may be playing at home. Even if they aren't, it's still worth visiting the **Olympic Stadium** (open to visitors 8.30am– 6pm; November to March, 9am–4.30 pm). At the south end you can learn quite a lot about the Bavarian mentality but if this sounds too risky, and you don't relish the

thought of singing along to 'ole, ole, ole, ve are ze chempions' stick to the stadium tours on offer. In the innards of the stadium, activities from body building and gymnastics to yoga are open to anyone in the **Health Park (Gesundheitspark**; Monday, Wednesday, Thursday, 2–10.30pm; Tuesday, Friday, 6–10pm).

If you're already fit, you can stroll through the park, take pictures, sunbathe, eat ice-cream and climb up the '**Olympic Mountain**', made of World War II rubble: you'll be rewarded with a fine view from the top.

As you cast your gaze around, you're bound to notice the silver silhouette of a Russian-style church to the west, peeping at you over a garden fence. This is the **Ost-West-Kirche (East-West Church)** of Oberwiesenfeld. It's the work of the 'Olympic Hermit', Timofei Prochorov. Papa Timofei is Russian by birth, looks like Rasputin

The Ost-West-Kirche

himself and has attained—according to his own record—the biblical age of 95.

'One night the Mother of God appeared to me and said, "Go to the West and build a church".' This is his explanation of why he came to Munich in 1953. Without first obtaining the necessary planning permission, Prochorov erected the East-West Church, plus a cottage to live in, on State land. For him, the wooden, Russian-style church with its onion domes and unique metal foil interior, is the symbol of mankind's single, unified 'religion'.

Officialdom finally 'discovered' Timofei in 1972 and immediately tried to have the holy 'squatter' forcibly removed. But mass protests by the public made him a local hero, eventually winning for him the right to lifetime occupancy of his unique structure. Visitors are usually welcome and sometimes manage to engage him in conversation. He also welcomes donations to the church, or towards his own modest needs.

Rudolf-Harbig-Weg will take you to Schwere-Reiter-Straße and Leonrodplatz, where you can catch a tram, bus or taxi back to the bustle of the city centre.

7. An Afternoon of Art

A tour of Munich's museums.

—u2 Theresienstraße or Königsplatz, Taxi to *"Alte Pinakothek"*—

When my mother comes to visit me in Munich, it usually rains. This never bothers her: "We'll go to the museum!" she beams. And there are certainly enough of them to choose from. Forty-six state, municipal and private collections are enough to keep anyone busy for quite a number of rainy afternoons. Museums of great art, sewing machine museums, the Deutsches Museum . . . the rain never lasts so long that you have to look at the same thing twice.

First on the list, of course, is a visit to one of the world's six leading art galleries, the **Alte Pinakothek** (open 9am–4.30pm every day except Monday; also 7–9pm Tuesday and Thursday), on the corner of Barer Straße and Theresienstraße (U-Bahn Theresienstraße). It was built between 1826–36, in the style of the Italian High Renaissance, from plans by Leo von Klenze, and gives an impression of greatness and peace even from the outside. When you go up the mighty staircase, you feel very small and insignificant by comparison.

The Alte Pinakothek is especially famous for its immense Rubens rooms, full of voluptuous, intertwining female bodies which seem to overflow the frames of the pictures, Albrecht Dürer's gorgeous *Four Apostles*, and the obsessive detail of Albrecht Altdorfer's *Battle of Alexander*, all a feast for the eyes. If these works aren't your cup of tea, continue to the Dutch School—to Rembrandt, Frans Hals or

Pieter Breughel—or let yourself be captivated by the colours of Titian, Raphael and Tinteretto.

By comparison, the **Neuen Pinakothek** (New Pinakothek) appears positively cheerful (9am–4.30pm every day except Monday; also 7–9pm Tuesday). The museum, built in 1981, leads the visitor through a maze of rooms containing paintings from the 19th century. Gauguin's beautiful *Nativity* made a particular impression on me. And the architect even remembered to include a café and a fountain. Don't hurry through this afternoon, rainy or not. Take your time, either here or in another museum. There's the **Städtische Galerie (Municipal Gallery)** in the **Lenbachhaus**, for example, once the town villa of the 'painter prince' Franz von Lenbach (10am–6pm every day except Monday). Here you'll find the works of the Blue Rider School, together with *Zeige Deine Wunde* (Show Your Wound), by Josef Beuys, which caused a furore when it was first shown. The Lenbachhaus is on the corner of Luisenstraße and Königsplatz (U2).

In the **Glyptothek** (10am–4.30pm every day except Monday; 12.30–8.30pm Thursday) and the **Antikensammlung** (Collection of Antiquities) (10.30am–4.30pm every day except Monday; noon–8.30pm Wednesday) opposite, both on Königsplatz, are all the Greek and Roman works collected (liberated? filched?) by Ludwig I. This is one of the major collections of its kind in the world complete with . . . a café.

You'll need at least half a day for the **Stadtmuseum** (Municipal Museum, 10am–5pm every day except Monday; 10am–8.30pm Wednesday). Exceptional exhibitions on special themes (eg 'Death' or 'The Isar') complement permanent exhibitions on the city's history, photography and film. The **Villa Stuck** at Prinzregentenstraße 60 (Tuesday–Sunday 10am–5pm; Thursday till 9pm) documents the turn of the century with exhibits of the life and work of the "painter count" Franz von Stuck. At times it has excellent special exhibitions.

Right at the top of my list of 'musts' is the **Valentin-Museum** in Isartor (Monday, Tuesday, Saturday, 11.01am–5.29pm; Sunday, 10.01am–5.29pm). Here you *must* pay your respects to Karl Valentin, master of language, Dadaist and real life Godot. Bow down before wacky artefacts and relics displayed as though in a shrine. Also in Isartor is, by my lights, the best café in town, slumbering peacefully and almost undisturbed.

Finally, visit the **Künsterwerkstatt** (artist workshops, Lothringestraße 13, 1–7pm), one of the few places in Munich where you can see modern art and meet the artists. Afterwards, you really ought to . . . but, then again, the rain in Munich never lasts long enough for you to explore all the treasures the city has to offer. You'd have to schedule your visit to coincide with fine weather only.

8. Traces of History

A tour of Old Munich: Viktualienmarkt, Stadtmuseum (Municipal Museum), Sendlinger Straße, Asam Church, Kreuzstraße.

—u-Bahn 3/6, s-Bahn Marienplatz, Taxi to "Viktualienmarkt"—

This half-day tour begins right at the heart—stomach?—of Munich, the Viktualienmarkt. This location is unbeatable for its ultra-Bavarian local colour, which lives on despite, or because of the steady streams of tourists. Wellbeing is ensured by various stands, pubs and cafés located around the market, the **Café du Marche** for instance, or the Indonesian-Thai **Halim** in the Frauenstraße.

After a little something to eat or drink, the next stop is **Prälat-Zistl-Straße** along the Sebastianblock. If you turn right at the next small junction, you'll find the **Munich Municipal Museum (Stadtmuseum)** at **St-Jakobs-Platz**.

This square, so full of tradition, where the Jakobi-Dult fair was held from the 14th century onwards (now held at Mariahilfplatz in the Au), is now a gaping wound in the heart of the city. Its predicament isn't really solved by the **Stadtmuseum**—worth seeing, but bursting at the seams. The reconstructed former armoury is crammed

The Stadtmuseum

with a historical museum and museums of puppetry, film and photography, all jostling for space. The **Café im Stadtmuseum** is rated one of *the* places to be, especially in the evenings. You can easily spend the whole afterrnoon there—and the whole evening in the **Filmmuseum** (Tuesday–Sunday, 11am–midnight; Monday, 4pm–midnight).

When you leave the museum, St-Jakobs-Platz seems twice as terrifying as it did before, which is good enough reason to turn right as fast as possible, go up Oberanger as far as Rosental, and head left down Rosental into **Sendlinger Straße**. Trying to cross Rosental before this point should only be attempted by sprinters or anyone tired of life. If you've had enough, you can catch up on your shopping in Sendlinger Straße. Small specialist shops, friendlier than the elegant snobs' shops in Theatinerstraße, or the frantic Kaufinger/Neuhauserstraße, give this old street its character.

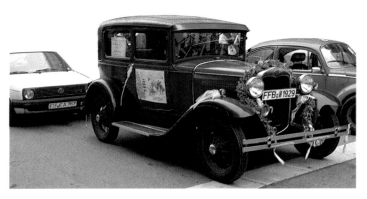

After the offices of the *Süddeutsche Zeitung* and the *Abendzeitung* newspapers, there's hidden treasure on the right among the trappings of commerce. The **Asamkirche**, an opulently ornamented rococo church designed by the Asam brothers, is a shock to the senses, if you like, but also a place of peace and contemplation.

After the Asampassage, with the **Asamhof** court, we come to Kreuzstraße. Neither the architecture nor the inhabitants of this super-trendy court fit into the rest of the area, and rocketing rents have resulted from brainwashing people into believing that living in the old part of the city is proof of Being Somebody. Still, this attitude has given the court a few cafés and a restaurant of Munich's **Bella Italia** chain.

Right from Kreuzstraße you plunge into the old almshouse quarter, only recognizable nowadays by the names: Josephspital, Herzogspital. It's interesting to note that this area, once so famous for its charitable and ecclesiastical institutions, is now largely given over to the horizontal profession as practised in rip-off joints. This weird juxtaposition has led to a strange mixture of Christian bookshops and municipal undertakers, artists' supplies and rather different sorts of 'supplies'. From Herzogspitalstraße, **Damenstift-straße** (which becomes Eisenmannstraße further down) leads back to the shoppers' paradise of Kaufingerstraße. And hospitality is absent too—or nearly: the **Augustiner** restaurant and beer hall still uphold the traditions of Munich hospitality, and the beautiful hall, with its shell-shaped ceiling, is the ideal place to mourn the passing of the 'good old days' over a glass of what is universally acknowledged to be Munich's finest beer.

Once Munich's 'liquid bread' has put some colour back in your cheeks, it's off towards Stachus on the last leg of the tour, with a superior feeling of having been initiated into some of the city's secrets. If you've managed to collect a few shopping bags on your travels, you'll probably allow yourself a taxi back. Otherwise, the U-Bahn, S-Bahn and tram are all at your service.

In the Augustiner beer hall

9. Little Versailles

An afternoon in the palace of Elector Maximilian II Emmanuel: in the Lustheim Palace with its great porcelain collection, the New Palace (Neues Schloß) with the art gallery, the Old Palace (Altes Schloß) with its gallery of religious paintings, and a visit to the Royal Bavarian Aircraft Hangar.

—s-Bahn 1 to Freising, Oberschleißheim station; taxi ("*Oberschleißheim Schloß*"), about DM35 from Odeonsplatz; by car from Odeonsplatz: Ludwigstraße–Leopoldstraße–Ingolstädterstraße, straight on and follow signs for Dachau/Oberschleißheim—

It's not easy to reach the palaces at **Schleißheim** by public transport, which is logical, if you consider that, at the end of the route are the homes of the aristocracy—folks who never have to take a bus. There's a 15–20-minute walk from the s-Bahn station, or you can wait for the 292 bus. But it's worth the trouble. Even my old friends from anarchist days in Berlin were enchanted by this miniature Bavarian Versailles built on the command of the "Blue Elector", as the ambitious general Maximilian II was known to the common people. He could be found in the front line during the battle for Vienna and was Supreme Commander of the western armies from 1688. Unfortunately, he backed the wrong side—France under Louis XIV—in the Spanish War of Succession, and was soundly beaten by the Duke of Marlborough and Prince Eugen at Höchstedt. This defeat put paid to his hopes of becoming emperor; and the only surviving fragments of that dream are the New Palace and Lustheim.

The fact that the New Palace will be undergoing extensive renovation until 1995 and that most of the famous collection of baroque masterpieces is closed, simplifies the decision about which museum to devote your energy to. The choice lies between the porcelain collection in Lustheim and the religious art in the Old Palace.

Logic recommends visiting Lustheim first, taking a quick look at the New Palace next and saving the Old Palace till the end of the tour. This logical progression means that at the end you haven't got far to go to the Palace pub. Sterner souls can inspect the Royal Bavarian Aircraft Hangar afterwards. For now, we'll only glance at the Old Palace and then turn right, with the Old Palace behind us, past the New Palace and into the palace gardens.

About a kilometre down the central canal lies **Lustheim**. This little palace was inspired by the Palazzo Madama in Rome, and is a real gem. The ceiling frescoes are among the earliest of Bavarian Baroque, and gave the chance of earning a living to a whole crowd of itinerant artists, mostly Italians, who had chosen Europe as their stamping ground. That's the most striking feature of Lustheim, in fact—its light, airy Mediterranean feel. The unique collection of porcelain, including many pieces from Meissen, makes Lustheim a special treat for enthusiasts.

Back towards the **New Palace**, the visitor can admire the absolutist dreams of Maximilian II—or as much of them as are on view to the general public (see above).

The **Old Palace**, converted at the beginning of the 17th century from a dairy farm to a small palace, has been given over to religious naïve art, an exhibition clearly expressing the devotion and faith of the artists.

The Deutsches Museum plans to move its Air and Space Travel section from the Museum Island site, to the newly restored **Royal Bavarian Aircraft Hangar (Flugzeugwerft)** south of the Old Palace, as a commemoration of the aeronautical pioneer Otto Lilienthal. Worth visiting when it's done, but meanwhile it's off to the **Schloßwirtschaft** pub or, if you'd rather, to the Greek restaurant **Poseidon** in Mittenheimerstraße.

Now all you have to do is to find yourself a taxi, and it's probably easiest to order one from the Central Taxi Switchboard in Munich, Tel: 21611.

Lustheim Palace

10. Shadows of the Past

Dachau: visit to the town followed by tour of the former Concentration Camp.

—S-Bahn 2 to Petershausen, alight at Dachau; to the camp: 722 bus to Robert-Bosch-Straße or 720 bus to Ratiborer Straße and 10mins walk; by car: Dachauerstraße, Karlsfeld, Dachau, follow signs; Taxi *"KZ-Gedenkstätte"* or *"Dachauer Schloß,"* DM40—

"I went to Dachau on an August evening with a friend. As we came up the hill and saw the market square with its gabled roofs spread before us in a peaceful evening mood, a powerful desire to live in that peace overcame me..." Such was Ludwig Thoma's description of his first visit to Dachau. Today, Dachau is associated with completely different impressions, and the deeds of unbelievable cruelty and inhumanity committed there; a town torn between the desire to forget all about its past and the hesitant attempt to come to terms with the shadow on its name and history.

Dachau was founded in 5BC by the Celts, then ruled by the Romans, by the Bishop of Freising in 805 (when it was named Dahaus) and, finally, by the Wittelsbach family. In the mid-18th century the place

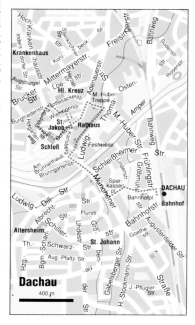

61

experienced an artistic invasion; painters in particular 'discovered' the countryside around this market town. Carl Spitzweg, Max Liebermann, Lovis Corinth arrived, and Dachau became the most important artists' colony, after Worpswede, in Germany.

Turf cutting and the growth of industry changed the character of the city. In World War I, a munitions factory gave employment to thousands of workers. And then came the Nazi period, when Himmler turned the buildings of this very factory into the first Nazi concentration camp. Between 22 March 1933 and 29 April 1945, over 200,000 prisoners were registered in the camp and over 32,000 of them met their deaths in various horrific ways. On 28 April 1945, some of the town's inhabitants and escaped prisoners attempted to flush out the camp's officers, who had barricaded themselves inside: the attempt ended in a bloodbath. Today, 34,000 people live with the burden of these past events.

Two buses run from Dachau S-Bahn station to the Concentration

St-Jakobskirche at Dachau

Camp (see above). If you are only interested in visiting the camp, you can go straight there.

Down **Langhammer Straße**, past idyllic rows of houses and over a little wooden bridge, you will come to Sparkassenplatz on Münchner Straße, with its attractive cobblestones. Turn right into Münchner Straße, past a lovely old bookshop, and continue along the Mühlbach until Martin-Huber-Treppe, a footpath bordered with trees, leads off to the left and into the heart of the old town, to **Konrad-Adenauer-Straße**. Up on the left on the corner is **Café Brüller**, with an inviting breakfast menu and a patio (Tuesday–Saturday, 9am–6pm; Sunday, 11am–6pm). Follow Adenauerstraße to the left. Here there are nicely painted houses and a square at the end which is straight out of a village idyll. Another possibility as a stopping place is the 17th-century **Brauereigasthof Zieglerbräu**.

Works of the **Dachau Artists' Colony** can be seen on the door of the Sparkasse Bank opposite (Wednesday, Friday, 10am–4pm; Thursday, 2–6pm; Saturday, 11am–5pm; Sunday, 1–5pm). A little further on, the pedestrian can examine the **Rathaus (Town Hall)**, an interesting combination of glass and concrete with older buildings. Cross Karlsberg and head down the Schloßgasse, where souvenirs are sold in a tiny old customs house with blue-and-white shutters. The **District Museum** opposite (Bezirksmuseum) has exhibitions on Dachau's history, crafts and traditional costume.

Only one of the original four wings of **Dachau Castle** has been preserved, which doesn't affect the marvellous view of Munich and the surrounding countryside in the least. Unfortunately, the castle is only open from May to September (and then only Saturday/Sunday from 2–5pm); at other times, only concertgoers can enjoy this masterpiece by the baroque architect Joseph Effner, who was responsible for the conversion of the Renaissance castle, built between 1558–73. To catch at least a glimpse of the interior, you can visit the **Castle Café (Schloßcafe**, 9am–6.30pm every day except Monday). If the weather's fine, you'll naturally prefer to sit in the beer garden behind the café.

From Schloßstraße you come to **Augsburger Straße**, Dachau's busy shopping centre. Pfarrgasse and Apothekergasse will take you back to the Town Hall, where you can get the No. 720 bus back to the s-Bahn or out to the **Concentration Camp** (KZ-Gedenkstätte, literally 'memorial'). At first, apprehension grips the visitor, followed by sheer horror. Words are inadequate. The only crumb of comfort is to be found in the large numbers of people from all over the world—most of them young— who feel drawn to this memorial. Many of them leave in silence, with an unspoken question on their faces: How could such a thing have been possible? All around there is the lush landscape, the brightness and colour of Munich, the normality of everyday life in Dachau. Here, on the other hand, looms an abyss, pure horror in black and white, a festering wound in German history—in the history of all mankind. Can these crimes ever be forgiven? Can the wound ever heal? (Open 9am–5pm; not advisable for children.)

11. Bavaria, Beer and Clowns

The Bavarian Hall of Fame, tour of Westend, Munich's 'outlands', the brewing district on both sides of Hackerbrücke, Zirkus Krone, visit to the Löwenbrauerei brewery.

—U4/5 Theresienwiese, Taxi to "*Bavaria*"—

No visitor to Munich would want to miss paying a visit to that Mighty Miss (Ms?), the **Bavaria statue**, and her worthy Bavarian 'mates' in the Hall of Fame. Here, where at certain times of the year, hundreds of thousands of people mill and throng (see section on the Oktoberfest) the wind sweeps across the bare wastes of Theresienwiese and up the Mighty Miss' skirt. Bavaria is a particularly impressive example of the bronze founder's art. One hundred and twenty or so steps up inside this hollow colossus bring you into the lady's head, which affords a fine view of the surrounding city and countryside.

Back on the ground, turn left up **Theresienhöhe**. If lunch is foremost in your mind, the **Hacker-Keller**, just ahead in the bottom layer of that concrete block, offers straightforward, honest Bavarian food. It's more interesting, though, to make a detour down **Ligsalzstraße** and **Tulbeckstraße** (left at Messeplatz, Kazmairstraße) where the **Ligsalz** pub (11am–1pm, Saturday 5pm–1am) and the exquisitely stylish **Speise Café West** (10am–1am) bear witness to the advancing tide of Yuppiedom even in the 'outlands' of Munich. If you like, you can prolong the walk down Gollierstraße to **Gollierplatz** (left here into Bergmannstraße, right into Tulbeckstraße). Westend is Munich's foreigners' quarter,

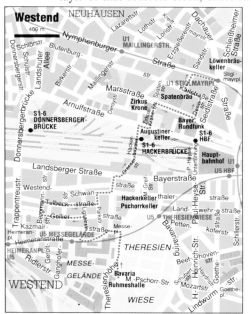

and you can get a taste of the colourful 'kebab' atmosphere while walking along—not a bad preparation for the rapidly thickening beer fumes. At the end of Tulbeckstraße, go left into Parkstraße, right into Schwanthalerstraße, and left into **Holzapfelstraße**. Now you're in the heart of the brewing district. On Landsbergstraße to your left you can see where **Augustiner** brews its *Edelstoff* beer (literally 'noble stuff') within ancient, exhausted walls. (You may be amused to know that beer was first developed by medieval monks to be drunk—for strength—during the long, Lenten fast.) Opposite, on the right, by the railway tracks, is the site of what is soon to be a new business centre

And now you're on **Hackerbrücke**. On clear days, the towers of the Cathedral appear to float right over the Hauptbahnhof. Right at Arnulfstraße is the opportunity to partake of refreshment (if the culinary delights of Westend didn't appeal to you) in the venerable, shady **Augustinerkeller**. You can sit where you like under the ancient chestnuts, but don't try to sit at the 'VIPs' table', reserved for bigwigs holding court.

If it's too early for an afternoon beer, why not visit Munich's resident circus, **Zirkus Krone** (left from the street of the same name). This is the only circus in Germany to have its own winter quarters, with animal enclosures, workshops and a small zoo. The cantilevered circus dome is used as a concert hall the rest of the time. One hundred and eighty-three metres (200 yards) to your right in Marsstraße are the huge copper vats of the Spaten brewery, gleaming in the sun through long windows. At 6am, fleets of lorries roar around here, transporting the 'water of life' to the waiting thirsty.

Towards town along Marsstraße, turn left into Denisstraße, then left again into Karlstraße and right into Sandstraße, where you can see the vats of the **Löwenbrauerei** brewery (tours on request, Tel: 520 04 96). Their end product can be sampled in the **Löwenbräukeller** (right at Nymphenburgerstraße).

Another stronghold of the hop-juice, this building was burnt out completely in 1986 and faithfully restored. It's the last building to

The Hackerbrücke bridge

remain unchanged, albeit only externally, on the whole of **Stiglmaier-platz** which, if old pictures are to be trusted, must have been one of the finest squares in Munich. Nowadays it's a prime example of inner city destruction and 'concrete restoration'. So drink up your beer and let's continue down Briennerstraße to Königsplatz. In Luisenstraße to the left of the Propylaea, you may decide to pay a visit to the **Lenbachhaus** art gallery (10am–6pm; Thursday till 8pm; closed Monday), but after those beers you're probably no longer in a fit state to look at museums.

At Königsplatz you can either take the U-Bahn back for a well earned rest, unless your feet are still up to a shopping foray after all that walking. If so, the grandiose **Elisenhof** (Luisenstraße towards Hauptbahnhof), formerly the premises of the venerable hotel Schottenhamel, will enable you to round off your shopping with a visit to the cinema.

12. Oktoberfest

At the 'Wies'n'.

—U-Bahn 4/5 Theresienwiese, S-Bahn Hauptbahnhof/Hacker-brücke, Taxi *"Wies'n Haupteingang"*, *"Bavaria"* or *"Esperanto"*—

At this point I prefer to leave all comments to a neutral observer, the author Thomas Wolfe and his hero Monk, and limit myself to a few interpolations based on my own experience, which only bear

out what Thomas Wolfe wrote in the 1930s.

"...at last he was to come close to the heart of this people—as if, after a voyage through the old barbaric forest, he would come suddenly upon them at their altars in a cleared ring." With that, Monk and Heinrich Bahr set off from the station to the Theresienwiese, on one of the three Wies'n Sunday afternoons. The last is the quietest day for a visit, and it's best if you start off in the morning (11am) so that you've had your fun by 6pm.

"There were dozens of booths and sheds filled with cheap dolls, teddy bears, candy wrappers, clay targets, etc, with all the accompanying claptrap as well as all the elaborate machinery for making one dizzy..." We won't bother listing all the nostalgic attractions like the flea circus or Schichtl's 'real live' executions. Nowadays, as then, dizziness is still the state to aim for.

"Late afternoon had come; Over all the Fair there rose the dense and solid fabric of a hundred thousand voices. Heinrich . . . taking Monk by the arm . . . joined in the vast oscillation of the crowd that jammed the main avenue of the carnival in an almost solid wedge." They try to find a place in the Ochsenbraterei, the Oxen Roastery. "The place, after the chill bite of the October air, was warm, warm with a single unmistakable warmth: the warmth generated by thousands of bodies crowded together in an enclosed place... At hundreds of tables people were sitting together devouring tons of flesh together with the great stone mugs that foamed with over a liter of the cold and strong October beer... Many of them stared at the people around them in a kind of stupefaction, as if they had been drugged. And indeed the air itself... was so thick and strong it could be cut with a knife..." But there was no room for Monk and Heinrich in the Ochsenbraterei, nor in the Löwenbräuhalle: "...they saw that it would be impossible to find a seat there. Thousands of people were roaring over their beer at the tables, and hundreds more milled up and down incessantly, looking for an opening."

At this point I'd like to present a short guide to the tents and beer halls:

SCHOTTENHAMEL, the oldest established Wies'n landlord, has beer from the Spatenbrewery. The opening ceremony takes place here, with well-known figures from politics, economics and show business sitting in the 'Town Hall box'. Here, you'll find the most civilised atmosphere of all the tents.

WINZERER FÄNDL, the Paulaner hall, has a reputation for having the best atmosphere. The music drives the people wild. (It was here that I last danced on a table, years ago.)

AUGUSTINER features the best beer—of course—and the most typically earthy waitresses and waiters.

FISCHER VRONI: there's no need to worry about beer sales with all that salty fish.

HOFBRÄUZELT has been the favourite of Anglo-Saxons for years. Here, you'll see Aussies, Kiwis and Brits dancing on the tables. The of official language is English. (Waitress: "You want a *Maß*? Eight mark costs.") The brass band struggles against the rugby and football choirs, and bouncers wrestle with the guests in an attempt to establish order.

ENTENBRATEREI, the Duck Roastery, is the best place for duck with red cabbage and dumplings at lunchtime. Reserve a table.

HIPPODROM, which uses trotting the horses around as an excuse to serve beer, and KÄFER—for trendy trad-costumed wearers of the Loden uniform—are licenced to stay open till 1am.

At last, Heinrich and Monk managed to find a place which, by the way, is next to impossible in the evening because of the high percentage of reservations. The best idea is to sit in the garden outside one of the tents. "And at last, dead center of that roaring tumult, they seated themselves triumphantly and immediately ordered two litres of dark beer and two plates of *schweinswürstl* (pork sausages) and *sauerkraut*. The band was blaring forth the strains of *Ein Prosit! Ein Prosit!* and all over the room . . . people . . . roared out the great drinking song and swung and rocked rhythmically back and forth. The effect of these human rings all over that vast and murky hall had in it something that was almost supernatural and ritualistic . . . something older . . . something that had swayed around an altar, and had made a human sacrifice..."

The hall echoes and thunders, Monk almost faints, and then, when, he is caught up in the chain of swaying people, he sings, shouts and laughs.

"There were no barriers any more. They drank and talked and ate together." At around 10pm (the Oktoberfest closes at 11pm) the tent begins to empty, Monk and Heinrich bid their new found friends farewell and wander through the streets in the best of spirits: "...far away, like time, like the ceaseless and essential murmur of eternity, the distant, drowsy, wavelike hum of the great Fair... They felt the sense of . . . a world invisible . . . of imminent and impending happiness, of impossible delight, that was almost theirs... And they went home."

I can add no more except to suggest that you follow Thomas Wolfe's characters and wend your way home, either on foot or by U-Bahn. Taxis are scarce after 10pm.

13. Neuperlach

Proof that life in Munich embraces more than just museums, palaces and beer gardens.

—U2/5 to Neuperlach Zentrum. Taxi to 'PEP Einkaufszentrum'—

The other—and down—side of the glamorous metropolis most tourists see is Neuperlach. Here, 60,000 people are stacked in 'test tubes' stranded on green lawns. High-rise blocks predominate on a bleak skyline. High crime and suicide rates here are the predictable result of the short-sighted architectural and urban housing policies of the 1960s.

These days, the grey prognosis has been tempered somewhat, since Neuperlach does have *something* to offer, not least affordable accommodation. Since the U-Bahn opened a fast link with the city centre, the huge, bright shopping centre here has developed into one of the best places to shop in Munich, and a variety of service industries have provided jobs on the doorstep. Neuperlachians have no need now to feel hard done by in their concrete world crisscrossed by four lane highways.

If you come in by U2 or U5 to Neuperlach Zentrum, your possibilities as pedestrians are automatically limited in this still 'car friendly' area. Leave the station, go towards Thomas-Dehler-Straße (West) and you'll find **PEP**, the shopping centre extensively rebuilt in 1989. It's a genuine alternative to the centre of Munich for shoppers, and easily reachable by car.

Before you load yourselves down with shopping bags, let's see how people live in Neuperlach. **Theodor-Heuss-Platz,** at the back of PEP (east exit), is surrounded by a huge circle of concrete with over 1,500 flats. This alone is worth a look, with all the surprising, moving attempts to bring a bit of human warmth into the block: phalanxes of trees, big fields and a playground where children lose their way, flowers, sunshades and wagon wheels on the balconies defy the anonymity of the area. At the ecumenical **Stefanszentrum** stands a 'Tree of Understanding', to encourage more contact with foreign neighbours (about 20 percent of the people in Neuperlach are foreigners). Housewives stand gossiping at the crossroads, so perhaps this place is a suburb after all…

Follow **Lüdersstraße** to Heinrich-Lübke-Straße, spanned by a bridge for pedestrians and cyclists, a rarity in this motorized town. On the other side is a different world: two-storey terraced houses along **Lorenz-Hagen-Weg**, dwarfed in the shadow of the concrete circle, lead to the old centre of Perlach. The road meets **Pfanzeltplatz** at St-Michael-Kirche. At the junction, an old house with wooden steps stands defying the (inexorable?) tide of new buildings. The baroque church dates from 1725. This and Pfanzeltplatz still have a touch of the village atmosphere of the *Peralohe* of old (Old High German for 'Bear Wood').

At the other end of Pfanzeltplatz you may stop for a rest in the hotel **Zum Bräu** (or the **Gasthof Zur Post** opposite). From here, the No. 39 bus will take you back around the concrete circle to Neuperlach Zentrum U-Bahn station.

After shopping, you can mix with the good citizens of Neuperlach in the **Michaelibad beer garden** in **Ostpark**. (By car, proceed to Albrecht-Schweitzer-Straße and then on to Heinrich-Wieland-Straße. By U-Bahn, get off at the Michaelibad station.) Over a beer, ponder what you've learned: living in Munich isn't automatically synonymous with Bogen- or Haidhausen, with art nouveau houses and the English Garden.

The PEP Shopping Centre

14. A Short Guide to Beer Gardens

Water is essential to life; but in Munich two other substances are considered just as essential, namely barley and hops. These have formed the basis of Bavarian beer since 1516.

The best time for me is a Sunday afternoon in the **Hofbräukeller** at Max-Weber-Platz. Outside the city, people are jostling and milling around by the lakes, but here all is peace and reverie. The beer stein gleams under the ancient chestnuts and a state of calm and serenity akin to paradise pervades everywhere. Once again I praise the day I discovered the Munich of beer gardens! There's no other place on earth with so many, one to suit every taste and enough to go around.

The most famous is undoubtedly the **Chinese Tower** (Chinesischer Turm) in the English Garden near Tivolibrücke. Much, much more than just a beer garden, the Chinese Tower is a parade of the vanities, a kaleidoscope of Munich, it *is* that *Liberalitas Bavariae* so often trumpeted in official speeches and which usually refers only to the speaker's own little world. When the beer counters are just opening at 11am and the sparrows hop around the tables eyeing the crumbs—that's when the Tower is at its most charming.

The largest and most traditional of all the Bavarian beer gardens—and so, we assume, in all the world—is **Hirschgarten** near Romanplatz, with its 8,000 seats. Families can find as much space as they need; children can ride on the carousel, play ball or look at the deer in the enclosure.

71

In Freimann, on Sondermeierstraße, is **Aumeister**, a popular destination for those wandering around the north of the English Garden. The guests represent every facet of that broad category, the 'blow-ins', which could be why the beer measures are so brazenly short.

You'll find two beer gardens in the centre of Munich alone, the somewhat faceless **Löwenbräukeller** at Stiglmaierplatz and the **Augustinerkeller** in Arnulfstraße, where Bavarian intellectuals (a small group indeed), literary types and artists rendezvous with their pals at the regulars' table. The remaining 5,000 places are taken up by the general public, often hailing from outside Munich.

The **Max-Emanuel-Brauerei** in Maxvorstadt is less 'big wigged' and easier to find your way around. Students from the nearby university give it its atmosphere.

A beer garden of a slightly different sort, with guests more from Bavarian alternative circles in winter is **Osterwaldgarten**, ten minutes from Münchener Freiheit. In summer, the pleasant little pub in Liebergesellstraße is overrun with the crowds from the nearby nightlife district.

The **Seehaus** on Kleinhesseloher See lake, in the middle of the English Garden, is eminently cultivated: snobs take the patio and duck lovers take the benches. It's lovely by day, crowded at night.

Taxisgarten in Taxisstraße in Neuhausen was run-down for years, then became the insiders' favourite, and is now given over to commerce. However, it's still less crowded than most beer gardens, and stays warm longer in the evenings because of the surrounding houses.

To the south on the Isar are three localities worth mentioning: the popular **Flaucher** in Thalkirchen, **Menterschwaige** in Harlaching and **Waldwirtschaft** in Großhesselohe. The latter two think they're a cut above the rest, probably because of their fine position on the banks of the Isar and the prosperity of the neighbourhood.

But perhaps you'll prefer the Hofbräukeller after all, where Hermann, the establishment's arch-waiter, lugs ten *Maß* glasses around at a time, bellowing 'What's wrong with you all? Have you stopped drinking?' If the neighbours complain about the noise, a court decision of 1985 states categorically that 'a beer garden is in the public interest.' Public interest, indeed: throughout the year Germans drink vast quantities of beer—about 160 litres (35 gallons) per person! So, bring another *Maß,* Hermann! We haven't stopped drinking, and you're only young once! (By the way, in summer all beer gardens close at around 1pm.).

15. Schwabing Nights

—u3/6 to Giselastraße. Taxi to 'Giselastraße'—

It's 10pm, and my visitors ask the question I've been dreading: 'What is there to do in Schwabing?' I twitch and explain that the era of 'Swinging Schwabing' is long gone, that the pavements around Münchener Freiheit are now awash only with tourists and young provincials. (Talk about rip-off joints and neon lights!)

But they're not to be put off, so we'll start at the corner of **Franz-Josef-Straße** and **Leopoldstraße**. On the left, heading out of town, you will see the neon lights of the well-known discotheque **Xeroi**, but the regular in-crowd who normally visit this establishment will only gather some time later. A bit further on, you'll see more flourescent lights glimmering in the night. This is the disco with the trendy name, **LA**, whose window display announces 'Dessous-clad go-go-dancing-girls on Friday and Saturday nights.' But you can do without all this and, as you have already eaten, the prospect of visiting either **Bologna** or **Princess Garden** is equally unappealing. Get yourselves in the mood with a cappuccino at **Café Venezia** (March to October, 9am to 1am), with its seats outside in the

Wedekindplatz

summer. A red neon sign on the other side of the road shouts **Roxy!**
Disregard the traffic and hurl yourselves across the road to this
yuppie heaven with its high-tech design and beautiful people.

On the way to **Münchener Freiheit** is **Leopold,** a perfectly normal
Bavarian pub looking a bit lost here. Opposite is **Café Servus**
(7am–3am).

At the Hertie block, which set the aesthetic standards of the
district for so long (chopped down to normal proportions at the
end of 1991), you come to the heart of everything usually associated
with Schwabing. And it's off into the pleasure dome, starting with
Feilitzschstraße: Broadway cinema, amusement arcade, pizza and
doner, pub following pub; **Route 66**, American diner, drinks and
small talk, Sundays open at 6am; **Alter Hut**, Vanity Fair, dental assistants and insurance agents smeared with layers of make-up;
Schwabinger Bierkeller, car dealers from the provinces with twirly
blond moustaches; **Hopfendolde**, pause for breath, no crowds, air!

On Siegesstraße, a ray of hope emerges on the right: **Haider's
Pizza**, with its 45 different kinds to take away! On **Wedekindplatz**
there's the **Drugstore** and a perfectly formed bar, **Peaches** (14 Feilitzschstraße)—pink make-up, pink cocktails and clouds of perfume.

Also in Feilitzschstraße: **Fatal, Käuzchen, Cocktail-Haus. Mutti
Bräu** (left into **Ursulastraße**) is a bit different for, since time im-
memorial, this has been the place to meet people. And the **Münchner
Lach- und Schießgesellschaft** (political/satirical cabaret; **Haim-
hauserstraße**, Tel: 391997) will give German-speakers something to
laugh about (booking essential).

On the way to Occamstraße there's **Har-
monika**, more or less unaltered since the
1960s and, in the building opposite, the
Theater am Sozialamt (Tel: 345890), one
of the few venues that dares to cause a stir
in Munich.

In **Occamstraße**: pubs, discos, pizzerias,
Stadtschreiber, Bar Nautic, Cockney, and
Circus Pils make no impression on the
memory; **Circo Valentino**—well, are you
too early, or are the others just late? Then

it's on to **Doctor Flotte**. Pubs like this are all the same, whether they're in Düsseldorf, Cologne or Munich. Is everybody happy, having a good time?

Albatros, Turbo Pils, Bierpavillon? Not worth mentioning. Then, **Schwabinger Brettl**—which used to be something. 'Live Music, cover charge DM5?'—you're not put off, but the place is deserted, and isn't that couple, Cindy and Bert, the German equivalent of Sonny and Cher? At last a ray of light: try to get into **Occam 24**— a jazz cellar featuring live Dixieland—where you can eat something at the little white tables, draped in classic, Bavarian beer garden style. Back out in the world of neon, you should avoid **Voyage**.

At the end of Occamstraße (in more ways than one), what now? Down **Artur-Kutscher-Platz** and into **Marschallstraße**. It doesn't need to be the **Wurzelsepp**, but what about the **Bijou**? From Marschallstraße turn left into **Marktstraße**, where No. 17 houses a rock bar called **Woodstock**, and next to it is the terrifying black door of **Roxx**. At the corner of Hesseloherstraße, the **Grünes Eck**, one of those timeless, normal pubs, brings back memories of the early 1970s. On the corner of Heimhauserstraße you can find French style in the newly opened **Le Bar Français**. The **Rock Café** has surprisingly good music, young people in casual everyday clothes and a friendly owner: balsam to your wounded sensibilities. In **Siegesstraße** again, **Haider's Pizza** claims your attention yet again, so you should forget **Vulcan**. Overpriced **Tomate**, on the other side, tries to do its bit for jazz. Don't weep any tears over **Krokodil** next door, but the **Schwabinger Podium**, on the corner of Wagnerstraße, is a worthwhile institution.

Now, enough is enough! It only remains for me to mention that **Adria**, corner of Leopoldstraße/Franz-Josef-Straße, will serve you food you can take a knife and fork to after 1am. And if you want any more, you can find it yourself.

Nights in Schwabing: a strong coffee at the Drugstore

16. Going Out in Haidhausen

—U-Bahn 4/5 to Max-Weber-Platz or Tram 18 to Wiener Platz.
Taxi to 'Wiener Platz'. There are *no* parking spots!—

Berliners can never understand why everything in Munich closes at 1am. This general closing time has been in existence for over 20 years, applies almost everywhere and especially to our destination tonight: Haidhausen. People are of two minds about closing times (a rumour is that they might soon be abolished) here in Schwabing's successor: the inhabitants can catch forty winks, at least after 1am, but pub owners and nightclubbers constantly complain.

A long night needs a solid foundation, so eat first. There's an attractive vaulted cellar at No. 6 Innere Wiener Straße called **Preysingkeller**, with its excellent wine list. If cuisine Française is more appealing, try the slightly alternative **Rue des Halles** at No. 18 Steinstraße, on Wiener Platz. Locate Italian food at **Il Museo** (Innere Wiener/Preysingstraße), Greek at **Kytaro** (36 Innere Wiener), crêpes at **Bernard and Bernard** (32 Innere Wiener), 'local colour' at **Hofbräukeller** (Wiener Platz) and vegetarian at **Amaranth** (Steinstraße/corner Milchstraße). You'll find Indian food at **Kashmir** (Pariser Straße 38, near Pariser Platz), and Turkish at **Merhaba** (9 Pariser Straße). But food isn't the only reason you're here.

Start the evening off with a *café au lait* and a look at the yuppie scene, nice and conspicuous behind the big windows of **Café Wiener Platz**. You can get a cocktail at **Harvey's Bar** (38 Innere Wiener Straße), although it may not come too swiftly.

On down **Steinstraße** and right into Preysingstraße, we find **Kuczinski** at No. 20, a prime example of the changes in the Haidhausen pub scene. This used to be a smoky jazz pub called **Vielharmonie**; now it's on the main Orient Express line, with pseudo-art nouveau, mirrors and indirect lighting. It has the nearby Gasteig cultural centre to thank for most of its clients. The owner of the alternative **Ansbacher Schlößl**, now **Kasino**, at the corner of Kellerstraße/Milchstraße draws from the Gasteig too.

Back on Preysingstraße, turn right into **Wörthstraße** for **Voila**, another super-stylish café, the successor to **Simbacher Hof**. In the summer the pavement outside is busy until 10pm. Off season, there's

77

subdued candlelight indoors. Next door, in the **Theater Rechts der Isar**, there's a pub of (almost) the old school and a stage for studio productions.

On Pariser Straße, go right to the **Paris Bar** in Gravelottestraße, or if you prefer, to **Café Größenwahn** in **Lothringer Straße**. Avantgarde cool and 'Berlin-style' years ago, nowadays it has a faintly old-fashioned air.

About now a few hunger pangs may be bothering you, so go on to **Rosenheimer Straße**, where on the right (towards the city, at No. 66) there's **Hooters**, an American-style bar and restaurant, or the upper class Greek **Pan**, opposite.

Our tour continues on the other side of Haidhausen, on the

corner of **Breisacher** and **Elsässer Straße**. **Juleps** is the local representative of the American bar culture which has spread through the city like the pox; **Café Cairo**, at the end of Breisacherstraße, is quite different, with a real live disc jockey and a pool table.

Lissabon, on the way, is a good place for a *café au lait,* although the big pub is so noisy that shouting is compulsory. Elsässer Straße offers the diametrical opposite, **Wiesengrund,** with classical music. Jazz aficionados will have to go a little further to hear off-beats: right out of Café Cairo to Orleansstraße and left to the **Unterfahrt,** still the place to hear the best musicians in town. The No. 19 tram takes you to Ostbahnhof station, where the last U- and S-Bahns (or taxis) can be got.

If you're not tired yet, try an encounter of the unforgettable kind. Go down **Kirchenstraße** towards town, keep straight on to Johannisplatz. Here **Johannis-Café** (11am–1pm, Friday and Saturday till 3pm, pictured above), although having lost some of its décor in the recent process of restoration, has been the meeting place for punks and peacocks, pensioners and ageing kings of swing for over 30 years, Charles Bukowskis and determined widows breaking down the barriers of age and class.

Haidhausen's other great curiosity is only for those who *really* stop at nothing. The **Blauer Engel** in **Wolfgangstraße** has no reputation to lose and loves it—it's probably the weirdest night- and strip-club in Germany. The décor is all Bavarian white and blue, with checked tablecloths, beery Bavarian ambience, and porn films (mostly cartoons) projected on the wall. The real high point, though, is the waitresses. As they bring your beer over, they start a clumsy striptease routine, arm in arm on the tables. It's so far removed from being erotic, so brutal and uninhibited, that . . . well, you sort of *have* to be there. ('Live' shows from 9pm.) After this, it really *is* time to go to bed.

17. Kir Royal

A stroll through Munich's night scene in the footsteps of the chic set, from solid fare followed by coffee on to a night, or nights, on the town at the city's most exclusive bars, clubs and discos—that is if the folks at the door will let us in.

If you want to venture into the chic set's den for an evening as one of the in crowd, you'd better dress warmly: you're likely to encounter a lot of cold, if chic, shoulders. Newcomers need a lot of coolness and the right outfit to avoid capsizing on their nocturnal expedition. All too often they'll end up on the wrong side of a closed door, or a determined bouncer. In Munich he's not there to throw people out, but to stop them going in in the first place, with a brusque shout of 'Regulars only!' Sometimes you may be lucky and turn into a regular on the spot. With careful preparation, we might manage it tonight.

You've all been to the hairdresser's, bought new clothes and shoes so, to get a feeling for what's required, eat first. At the huge **Peppermint Park LA** (51 Lilienstraße, 6pm–1am, Tel: 4801703) you don't stand out, but you should be able to tell from the waiter's behaviour whether you're cool enough. The **Juleps'** test (18 Breisacherstraße, 5pm–1am; Tel: 4480044) is stiffer, and it's wise to reserve a table if you want to order giant burgers and Mexican dishes here. If there's no joy at Juleps, try the in Greek pub **Pan** (98 Rosenheimer Straße, Tel: 488231).

Once you've got used to the chic atmosphere, it's a good idea to have a *café au lait* or a drink before your visit to the disco: it's expected of you, and does wonders for your coolness. Another spot is the new **Gorki Park** (Breisacherstraße) or the classic **Iwan** (15 Josephspitalstraße/19 Sonnenstraße, 11am–3am, Tel: 594933).

Now, at around 11.30pm, comes the moment of truth, and we set off on foot to the most sought-after disco in Munich: the **Park-Café** (7 Sophienstraße, 10.30pm–4am, Saturday till 8am).

The bouncer (usually the owner Hansi Grandl himself or his wife Inge) looks us up and down, we smile back coolly, expecting to be let in and—yes!—a nod, and we can enter the holy of holies. But our friends have to stay outside. Hansi doesn't like groups, so it's best to attempt entry in pairs at most, and better not alone. It's also important not to shove your way up to the door in the second or third row of a bunch of people. And if you don't make it, console yourself with the fact that VIPs sometimes fail the examination too. Maybe next time...

Inside, there are lots of mirrors, a big, crowded dance-floor, thumping loudspeakers and cool people in the in-crowd's uniform. You come in cool, you hang around cool, you go out cool—often without once opening your mouth.

If you failed the entrance exam—it's too early for discos, anyway—build up your self-confidence with a quick cocktail at **Schumann's** American bar (36 Maximilianstraße, Monday–Friday, 5pm–3am; Sunday, 6pm–3am). Municheans who have a high opinion of themselves look in here in the evenings; not only the in-crowd, but also arty types, politicians and intellectuals. If **Schumann's** is

too full (and this is the normal state of affairs), the alternatives are **Harry's New York Bar** (4pm–3am, closed Sunday, piano bar from 9pm, five minutes' walk away at 9 Falkenturmstraße) or the **Havana Club** (8pm–1am, Thursday–Saturday till 2pm, five minutes' walk away at 30 Herrnstraße).

Now it's time to try a disco again, this time **P1** (in the Haus der Kunst at 1 Prinzregentenstraße, midnight–4am) owned by Michael Käfer, the caterer's son. **P1** is the place where yuppies get rid of their fast bucks, surrounded by familiar faces, expensive drinks and chart music. If you fail the entrance test here, you're enough of an expert by now to try again at the **Park-Café,** but maybe **babalu** (Leopoldstraße 19, 11pm–4am) or the **babalu bar** (1 Ainmillerstraße, 9pm–3am) would be a better bet; or you could give up altogether and go to **Far Out** (2 Am Kosttor, next door to **Harry's Bar**), where a rare commodity is to be had: permission to go in.

Finally, there's only **Nachtcafe** left (9pm–6am). People, some older, some younger, collect to bop along to live music and ward off night-starvation. The bouncers are casual, so normal, less than ice cool types have a chance too.

And if they won't even let you in here, you might want to start asking yourself a few searching questions and seek oblivion in the nearby **Weißbierkeller** (1 Bayerstraße, Tuesday–Sunday, 3–7am; 8am–midnight; Monday 8am–midnight). Beer and solid Bavarian local colour, with the occasional punch-up, will cheer your troubled soul, and tomorrow morning the world will be back to normal, and *mir san wieda dahoam*—home sweet home.

Day Trips

18. Lakeside Idyll

A day trip to Ammersee lake: walk to Andechs Monastery, steamer trip to Utting and walk to Schondorf/Stegen with a chance to bathe.

—S5 to Herrsching. By car: Lindau motorway, exit towards Herrsching via Weßling, Seefeld. Taxi to 'Herrsching', around DM60—

There's a phrase which is music to the ears when Munich is the topic of conversation: 'high-value leisure'. And most people don't even mean the city itself, but the surrounding countryside which, as everyone knows, extends as far south as Tuscany, not to mention the Alps. Upper Bavaria has already been taken over by city-dwellers, who invade it at weekends as their God-given right.

Follow their example and take the S5 to the west. Your goal is Ammersee Lake, your starting point the town of Herrsching, about 40 minutes from Marienplatz.

You'll need a whole day for this two-part trip, and your starting time should be 9 am from Munich. Once you get to **Herrsching**, follow the signs to 'Heiliger Berg' (Holy Mountain), and the **Andechs Monastery**, one of the most visited places of pilgrimage in Bavaria. It was built in the 15th century on the site of the Count of Andechs' ancestral castle, and its early fame came from a collection of relics brought back from the Crusades.

The monks of Andechs have managed to combine piety and profit for the benefit of the Lord and their good selves. Of course you can gaze at relics here, attend concerts of classical and sacred music, and admire the view of the Five Lakes from the church tower. But

Andechs actually owes its popularity to—we're in Bavaria, after all—the fine beer of the monastery brewery. The monastery inn, the beer gardens, and the picturesque views of surrounding landscape all serve to enhance the somewhat unholy pastime of downing large quantities of traditional dark and light beer.

Still, the monks invented the stuff. Not allowed to eat solid food during Lent, they came up with a way of consuming their barley in fluid form. This tradition is still very much alive in Bavaria: a very strong, full-bodied beer is still brewed during Lent, though it's not recommended for anyone on a reducing diet. However, returning to the subject of Herrsching, there is a climb of around 1hr 45mins up to the holy mountain, and this may help you justify imbibing those extra calories. The trek itself is as worthwhile as the destination: along Kienbach Ri-

Andechs Monastery

ver, twisting and turning upwards under shady trees, until the steep steps which lead right to the church. Look at the church *before* you slake your thirst; then enjoy a beer and a Romadur cheese, watch the bustling crowds and head back to Herrsching for Stage Two, and the conquering of Ammersee! Don't worry, it's easy. Just board one of the steamers to take you all round the lake.

You should disembark at Utting, but not to look at the town. It's more interesting to set off straight away for Schondorf, or rather Stegen (about 6km, or 3.75 miles; two hours). After the **Alte Villa**,

with its lovely beer
garden on the lake, the route
leads past fine old houses, showing their
age, but all the lovelier for that. The western bank of
the lake is quite rural here, peaceful and tranquil and without that
hustle and bustle you find on Starnberger Lake. There are benches
everywhere and jetties projecting into the water, where you can sunbathe, windsurf or swim in this rather shallow lake, though much of
the lakeside is reserved for water fowl.

In **Schondorf**, probably the nicest place on the west bank, you
can stroll along the promenade and then enjoy a well earned rest in
the beer garden **Zur Post** next to the church. The view of the lake
glittering in the afternoon sun, a *Weißbier* and a snack are enough
to make you think you're in heaven. From Schondorf you can
return to Herrsching by boat (April to the end of September).

If you still have some strength left, you can continue along the
lake towards Stegen. The route is lined with little lakeside villas,
and you'll come to a nudist beach and **Stegen**, where you can take
the steamer back to Herrsching. When the blue mist rises in the
south to remind the mountains of the coming night, you'll certainly
understand what we Municheans mean by 'high-value leisure'.

Linderhof Castle

19. The Castles of the Fairytale King

Three day trips to the castles of Ludwig II: Linderhof, the rococo royal villa, Neuschwanstein, Germany's most famous castle where the king recreated Wagner's dream world, and Herrenchiemsee, the 'new Versailles'.

Royal castles in Bavaria automatically mean the 'Big Three'—Linderhof near Oberammergau, Neuschwanstein near Füssen, and Herrenchiemsee on Chiemsee Lake at Prien. All three were the product of the romantic imagination of Ludwig II, Bavaria's fairytale king (1845–86).

'The king is dead, long live the king!' shouted the Bavarians in March 1864 as the large and impressive figure of the 18-year-old crown prince, Ludwig, paced behind the coffin of his father, Maximilian II, en route to the family vault in the Frauenkirche. This sheltered youth, who had grown up in the isolation of the mountains around Hohenschwangau Castle, considered Louis XIV of France and composer Richard Wagner to be demigods, and these two figures were to be his inspiration in the construction of the dreamlike castles which draw so many to Bavaria each year.

But for Ludwig II, the last feudal builder of European history, the structures would spell doom. The castles not only ate up the whole of his private fortune, but also substantial sums from the state budget. Lavishness, his eccentric, homophile lifestyle, and his lack of leadership led to notorious proceedings which placed him under guardianship at the instigation of several ministers and royal relatives. On 8 January 1886 the king, without inquest, was diagnosed as suffering from a progressive mental disorder. After a short political struggle, he was removed to Berg and Starnberger Lake, where he met his end.

By now even the muddiest backwater in the States or Japan has heard of Ludwig, panegyrized by some as the Bavarian national

84

hero, vilified by others as a paranoiac with homosexual tendencies. His tragic end in Starnberg Lake can still provoke excited arguments in pubs even today: a) he drowned b) he drowned himself c) he was drowned d) someone heard a pistol shot. Whatever happened, the State of Bavaria has this isolated patron of the arts, generous sponsor of Richard Wagner and admirer of the French Sun King, to thank for a collection of magnificent buildings which attract millions of tourists every year and a concomitant number of German marks for the state coffers.

The simplest way to get to the castles from Munich is either to hire a car or to take one of the many organised bus tours (eg from ABR, the Official Bavarian Travel Agency, or Autobus Oberbayern). Public transport is also an option, but takes more time and trouble.

Linderhof

From Munich: **Train:** to Oberammergau (99km/61.5 miles, about two hours) and then bus: **Car:** Lindau motorway, Herrsching, Weilheim/Peißenberg, Rottenbuch, Oberammergau—or Garmisch-Partenkirchen motorway or Bundesstraße (federal highway) 2 to Oberau, then right via Ettal Monastery. **Opening times:** Summer, 9am–5.30pm; Winter, 9am–12.15pm and 12.45–4pm; for guided tours tel: 08822/512. **Entrance:** DM7 (DM6 in winter)

The route by car to Linderhof passes through particularly delightful scenery, past Andechs Monastery, Oberammergau and the impressive Ettal Monastery.

A trip to France inspired Ludwig II to tear down his father's hunting castle and build a 'new Versailles' in its stead. But the idea was not fulfilled, and a 'mere' royal villa was the result. The interior is in the rococo style. Of special note are the Hall of Mirrors and the movable dining table with genuine Meissner

Neuschwanstein Castle

porcelain flower decorations. Ludwig had the table fitted with a lift mechanism in order to be able to dine alone: the table was lowered into the kitchens directly beneath the dining room, and raised again filled with steaming dishes, in the best fairy story fashion. Visitors should not miss a walk through the gardens and a look at the oriental-style **Moorish Kiosk**, which Ludwig found at the World Fair of 1876 in Paris; the famous **Venus Grotto**, an artificial stalactite cave used as a stage set for Wagner's *Tannhäuser,* is also worth seeing. The grotto also contains a small lake and waterfall, both 'magically' illuminated in various colours by the first electric lighting plant in Germany.

Neuschwanstein

From Munich: **Train** to Füssen (131km/81 miles, about 2hrs), then bus. **Car** to Peißenberg, as the route to Linderhof, then Peiting, Steingaden, Schwangau. **Opening times:** Summer, 9am–5.30pm; Winter, 10am–4pm. Tel: 08362/81035. **Entrance:** DM8

No getting out of it, today it's Neuschwanstein. Ludwig made the bed, and now we have to lie on it once or twice a year with our visitors, so to speak. Even if we've done the tour in every language possible (the contents change with the language, and the English tour is worth the trip if only for the guide's Bavarian English and the sheer enthusiasm of the participants) we can't let our visitors go home without having seen Neuschwanstein.

The journey is lovely, with the chance of a detour in Steingaden or at the Wieskirche, that masterpiece of Bavarian rococo. Restoration work was finally finished in June 1991 and it is open to the public again. For your visit at Neuschwanstein arrive there shortly after opening time or just before closing to avoid long queues.

Germany's most famous castle stands 200m (657ft) above the valley floor. The king was convinced that the gods lived 'here with us on stony heights, with heaven's zephyrs all around,' as he wrote to Richard Wagner. That made Neuschwanstein the perfect place to recreate the dream world of Wagner's opera, a stage of stone for *Tannhäuser* and *Lohengrin.*

A visit to the Wartburg in Thüringen, where the medieval bards had competed in rhyme and music, gave him the idea for the place. So the centre of this pseudo-romantic palace is the **Sängersaal** (Bards' Hall) where frescoes depict the main plot of *Tannhäuser.* With its delicately coffered ceiling, candelabra and chandeliers, it occupies practically the whole of the fourth floor. It was a theatre decorator, not an architect, who first drew up this castle, but after 17 years in construction, Neuschwanstein was still not completed when Ludwig died.

The king didn't live long enough to enjoy this magnificent building to the full. For the most part, the décor on the third and fourth floors was completed in 1886, the year of his death. At the foot of the mountain there is ample opportunity to recover from your visit in a restaurant.

Herrenchiemsee

From Munich: **Train:** to Prien (87km/54 miles, about one hour), then bus to the pier and by ferry to the island of Herreninsel. **Car:** Salzburg motorway to Bernau, then Prien. To avoid traffic jams on the motorway: go via Ebersberg, Wasserburg, Amerand, Endorf to Prien. **Opening times:** Summer, 9am–5pm; Winter, 10.15am–15.45pm. Tel: 08051/3069. **Entrance:** DM8. On a summer's weekend, this trip features everything that Munich people thirsting for relaxation love least: traffic jams on the motorway, crowded beer gardens, crowded lakes! So, if you can, avoid weekends. Do something else, unless you want to know exactly how it feels to be a lemming.

On Herreninsel, Ludwig tried to achieve what he had failed to do at Linderhof: the construction of a new Versailles. In emulation of the French Sun King his ancestor Max II had once supported, he had a palace built as a romantic glorification of absolutist monarchy,

Herrenchiemsee Castle

at a time when the age of industrialization and mass democracy had well and truly taken over.

The castle's main room is the great Hall of Mirrors, which runs the whole width of the garden side and is 98m (321ft) long. Modelled on the Galerie des Glaces at Versailles, the mirrors, the 44 candelabra and 33 great glass chandeliers give the room an appearance of excess, truly the product of a fevered soul with delusions of grandeur (if the Society for the Preservation of the Memory of His Majesty Ludwig II will forgive me for saying so). As an antidote to the passion for splendour, which encourages melancholy musing, a walk around the island is called for to see the remains of the Benedictine monastery above the jetty and pass the time till the ferry sails from the beer garden with its view of the lake. Chiemsee is a paradise for all varieties of water sports: from pedalos to windsurfing, you can hire everything that floats here.

Dining Ex

What would a visit to Munich be without seeing a few genuine Bavarian pubs? Whether you take an active part in events *(zwoa, drei, g'suffa,* or one, two, three, down the hatch) or just watch passively, in the merry haze of beer the stomach's requirements shouldn't be neglected. An American has his steak, but a Bavarian has his pork, and you may only discover all the variations on pork there are here in Munich: roast pork, pig's trotters, pork belly, ribs, chops, liver, tripe, tongue. The rest of the poor pig is swept up, chopped up and reappears as pig's head brawn, pork sausages or *Leberkas*—literally 'Liver Cheese'— although it's common knowledge that it contains neither liver nor cheese. Only the world famous *Weißwurst*— white sausages—are an exception, made, mostly, anyway, of veal. Which part of the animal is a dark secret, and rightly so.

Nevertheless, a typical Munich day begins with *Weißwurst* for breakfast, best at the **Weißes Bräuhaus** in Tal, although every Munich native has his own favourite source for *Weißwurst*. It is supposed to be a sacrilege to order

them in pairs, these greyish-white sausages swimming in hot water. That's clear proof you're a tourist, and your waitress won't cast another glance your way. The question as to whether you eat the sausages with a knife and fork or with your fingers, with or without the skin, or whether you suck them out *(auszuzeln),* is a matter of hot discussion among experts, so that you have more or less free rein in this and need not worry about breaking taboos. However, sweet mustard is a must! As a liquid accompaniment, an *Affe* (literally, 'monkey'; dark, strong Aventinus Weißbier) is best—and you'd better have a couple of *Brez'n* rolls too, so that the day doesn't come to a complete standstill.

The pubs mentioned are, we feel, worth a visit because of their unique atmosphere. Everything is a matter of taste, so we won't pronounce judgement on the cuisine. You'll find more tips 'on the spot' in the tour descriptions.

The home of *Starkbier* (strong beer). The cult of beer swilling reaches unimaginable proportions here in spring: two litres of *Salvator* and you'll hear the angels singing.

Bavarian

AUGUSTINER
16 Neuhauser Straße, Tel: 55199257.
Daily, 10am–midnight.
Gorgeous old Munich brewery restaurant with fine interior.

DONISL
1 Weinstraße, Tel: 220184.
Daily, 8am–12.30am.
Traditional pub with a history of scandal (staff used to spike drinks with knockout drops, then pick guests' pockets), now renovated and harmless.

HAXNBAUER
5 Münzstraße, Tel: 221922.
Daily 11.30am–midnight.
The best grilled pork knuckles in town.

MAX EMANUEL BRAUEREI
33 Adalbertstraße, Tel: 2715518.
Daily, 11am–1am.
Perennially popular; salsa/lambada. Wednesday and Friday; Irish music Monday; Fasching dances; Bavarian rustic theatre; and a nice beer garden. Service sometimes a little slow.

SALVATORKELLER
77 Hochstraße, Tel: 4599130.
Daily, 9am–midnight.

WEIBES BRÄUHAUS
10 Tal, Tel: 299875.
Daily, 9am–midnight.
Supremely Bavarian; the best *Weiß-wurst* in Munich.

FRANZISKANER
5 Perusatraße, Tel: 231812.
Daily, 9am–midnight.
VIP Bavarian. Always crammed, especially so on Saturday mornings. In the evenings, stars are taken along on obligatory visits.

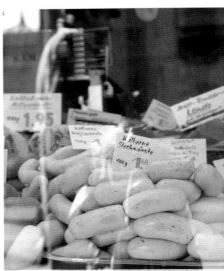

International

American

JULEPS
18 Breisacher Straße, Tel: 4480044.
Daily, 5pm–1am.

NEW ORLEANS
39 Orleansstraße, Tel: 4480520.
Daily, 11am–1am.
Down South Cajun. Y'all come, ya hear?

PEPPERMINT PARK LA
51a Lilienstraße, Tel: 4801703.
Daily, 6pm–1am; Sunday, 5pm–1am.
Thumping chart music and shouting guests at this huge neo-American restaurant.

Arab

ARABESK
86 Kaulbachstraße, Tel: 333738.
Daily, 5pm–1am; Sunday, 11am–2.30pm.
Brunch, belly dancing and music.

Chinese

There are over 60 Chinese restaurants in the city, none of whose Chinese cuisine we can really be proud of, according to my source (married to a Chinese). Some of them are good, but tend to pander to European tastes.

HONG KONG
Munich 40, Tengstraße 34,
Tel: 2716613.
One of the oldest in Munich; nice little garden.

ZUNG HUA
Munich 2, 33 Bayerstraße,
Tel: 555320 and 594939.
Daily, noon–3pm, 6–11pm.
Chinese rate this as the best in Munich. 'Barbarians' aren't treated quite as well.

French

LE CEZANNE
Munich 40, 1 Konradstraße,
Tel: 391805.
Daily, 6pm–1am.
Provençal dishes at reasonable prices; friendly service.

RUE DES HALLES
18 Steinstraße, Tel: 485675.
Daily, 6pm–1am.
Vachement bien!

QUARTIER LATIN
16 Konradinstraße, Tel: 657895.
Daily, 6pm–1am.
Friendly restaurant at moderate prices.

Greek

KYTARO
36 Innere Wiener Straße,
Tel: 4801176.
Daily, 5pm–1am.
Always full (book ahead), big garden at the back, live music.

PAN
98 Rosenheimer Straße,
Tel: 488231.
Daily, 5pm–1am.
Highest class Greek place in town.

TO STEKI
17 Schmellerstraße, Tel: 771610.
Daily, 5pm–1am.
My own Hellenic favourite.

Hungarian

Puszta Csarda
15 Volkartstraße, Tel: 168271.
Daily, except Monday, 6pm–1am

Indian

Sangam
27 Ehrengutstraße, Tel: 7257184.
Daily, 6pm–1am.
The only place you'll get Southern Indian *Masala Dosa*.

Noor Jahan
5 Kaiserstraße, Tel: 348009.
11am–14.30pm, 5.30pm–midnight.
Tastes almost like India.

Indonesian

Garuda
87 Theresienstraße, Tel: 525936.
Daily, except Monday, 11.30am–2.30pm, 6–11pm.
Try the Rijstafel.

Italian

Italy
108 Leopoldstraße, Tel: 346401.
Daily, 11.30am–midnight.
Lively Schwabing restaurant.

Pantera Rosa
Munich 80, Rosenkavalierplatz 15, Tel: 917132.
Daily, noon–3pm and 6pm–1am.
Fine food, patio.

Romagna Antica
52 Elisabethstraße, Tel: 2716355.
Daily, 11.30am–3pm and 6pm–1am.
Has kept up its quality for years; semi-VIP.

Tre Colonne
43 Hiltenspergerstraße, Tel: 2717246.
Daily, except Tuesday, noon–1pm and 6pm–midnight.
Nice cellar restaurant; quality of service varies.

Japanese

Daitokai
59 Kurfürstenstraße, Tel: 2711421.
Daily, except Sunday, noon–2.30pm and 6pm–midnight.
Food cooked at table. Lunchtime table d'hote affordable; evenings expensive.

Akasaka
3 Mariannenstraße, Tel: 293100.
Daily, except Sunday, noon–2.30pm and 6pm–midnight.
No frills; ideal for business meals.

Mexican

Pappasito's
44 Schraudolphstraße, Tel: 2721346.
Daily, 6.30pm–1am.
Tequila and tacos, high-class; surprisingly good.

Persian

Niawaran
18 Innere Wiener Straße,
Tel: 487408.
The 'local' for the Persian population.

Polynesian

Waikiki
39 Neureutherstraße, Tel: 2711146.
Daily, 7pm–2am.
Exotic cocktails.

Spanish

Centro Español
20 Daiserstraße, Tel: 763653.
Daily except Monday, lunchtimes, 5.30–10.45pm.

Book in the evenings. Good, hearty food; meeting place for many Spaniards.

Thai

SHIDA
32 Klenzestraße, Tel: 269336.
Daily, 6pm–midnight.
Often jam-packed; booking recommended—homage to the greatness of Thai cuisine.

Turkish

SCHWIMMKRABBE
13 Ickstattstraße, Tel: 2100080.
Daily, 5pm–1am.
Turkish-Kurdish pub. Friendly owner, good food —delicious starters; belly dancing most weekends.

Vietnamese

TIEN HUU
47 Theresienstraße, Tel: 522518

Daily, except Monday, 6pm–midnight.
Doctor Tien knows how to cook.

CODO
7 Lothringerstraße, Tel: 4485797.
Daily, 6–11pm
Tiny family business, could hardly be improved on.

Vegetarian

JAHRESZEITEN
9 Sebastianplatz, Tel: 2609578/79.
Daily, 7–11pm.
Tasty wholefoods all day. Cosy interior.

AMARANTH
42 Steinstraße, Tel: 4487356.
Daily, 11.30am–1am; Saturday, 5pm–1am.
High-class, bright, relatively expensive.

Gourmet

AUBERGINE
5 Maximilianplatz, Tel: 59 81 71.
Daily, noon–2pm and 7pm–midnight, except Sunday/Monday and public holidays.
Eckart Witzigmann, Munich's gourmet high priest, serves classic and nouvelle cuisine delicacies.

KÄFER-SCHÄNKE
1 Schumannstraße/corner Prinzregentenstraße, Tel: 4168-1.
Daily, 11am–midnight, except Sunday.
The restaurant of Munich's deli king.

LA MER
24 Schraudolphstraße, Tel: 2722439.
Daily, 7pm–1am, except Monday.
The fish here is excellent.

LE GOURMET
46 Ligsalzstraße. Tel: 503597.
Daily, 6pm–midnight.

TANTRIS
7 Johann-Fichte-Straße, Tel: 362061.
Daily, noon–3pm and 6.30–1am, Saturday kitchen closes at 10.15pm; closed Sunday, Monday and public holidays.

Student

ATZINGER
9 Schellingstraße, Tel: 282880.
Daily, 10am–1am.
Classic, established student pub.

BAADER CAFÉ
47 Baaderstraße, Tel: 2010638.
Daily 11-1am, except Sunday 10-1am.
Recommendable Sunday brunch.

CAFÉ IM STADTMUSEUM
1 St-Jakobsplatz, Tel: 266949.
Daily, 10am–midnight.

Going for a long time since it was founded by the painter Brum.

FRAUENHOFER
9 Frauenhoferstraße, Tel: 266460.
Daily, 4.30pm–1am, Sunday 10–1am.
Alternative stronghold.

RHEINPFALZ
35 Kurfürstenstraße, Tel: 2710698.
Daily, except Saturday, 6pm–1am.
Greying collection of made-good ex-1968ers.

RUFFINI
19 Munich, 22 Orffstraße,
Tel: 161160.
Daily, except Monday, 10am–midnight;
Sunday, 10am–6pm.
Home-made and home-baked delicacies from 'in' collective.

TAGÖLL
12 Hans-Sachs-Straße, Tel: 266821.
Daily, 8am–1am; Monday, 7pm–1am.
My local.

Late Night and Snacks

ADRIA
19 Leopoldstraße, Tel: 366529.
Daily, 10am–3am.
Your salvation after 1am in Schwabing; mixed clientele.

CAFÉ FRISCHHUT/SCHMALZNUDEL
8 Prälat-Zistl-Straße at Viktualienmarkt, Tel: 268237.
Daily, 5am–2pm, Saturday 5am–3pm.
Sober up in the small hours with local colour. Speciality: a kind of doughnut called *Auszogne* (literally, 'stretched-out'; applies only to doughnuts, not to guests).

CHARIVARI
92 Türkenstraße, Tel: 282832.
Daily, except Sunday and Monday, 9pm–3am.
What comes in after 1am has to be seen to be believed.

LA PIAZZETTA
3 Oskar-von-Miller-Ring, Tel: 282999.
Daily, 11.30am–6am.
Excellent Italian food, fine service; often full, fairly VIP.

NACHTCAFÉ
5 Maximiliansplatz,
Tel: 595900.
Daily, 9pm–5am.
Unavoidable heavies on the door, usually has good jazz.

Bars

HARRY'S NEW YORK
9 Falkenturmstraße, Tel: 222700.
Monday–Saturday, 4pm–3am.
Establishment with a long tradition.
Pianist from 9pm.

HAVANA CLUB
30 Herrnstraße, Tel: 291884.
Sunday–Wednesday 6pm–1am; Thursday–Saturday, 7pm–2am.
Crowded, but excellent service and interesting drinks.

SCHUMANN'S
36 Maximilianstraße, Tel: 229060.
Daily, except Saturday, 6pm–3am.
Amazing reputation, famous for unusual cocktails, interesting clientele.

Discos

BABALU
19 Leopoldstraße. Tel: 399451.
Daily, 8pm–4am.
Female bouncers and live performances.

MAXIMILIAN'S
31 Maximiliansplatz, Tel: 266515.
Daily, except Monday, 9pm–3am.
Ties preferred.

P1
1 Prinzregentenstraße, Tel: 294252.
Daily, 10.30pm–4am.
The best known of Munich's discos. If
your face is wrong you'll need Tina,
Mick, Prince *et al* to get in.

PARK-CAFÉ
7 Sophienstraße, Tel: 598313.
Daily, 6pm–4am.
The old game of trying to get in.

TANZCAFÉ GRÖSSENWAHN
43 Klenzestraße, Tel: 2016776.
Daily, 9pm–1am.
Bouncers only seldom. Special evenings
for minorities and weirdos.

Gay/Lesbian

KAROTTE
37 Reichenbachstraße, Tel: 2014294.
Daily, except Sunday, 6pm–1am.
Pleasant atmosphere, good food—says
my female informant.

MRS HENDERSON
1 Müllerstraße, Tel: 2604323.
Daily, except Monday, 9pm–1am.
A place for him to meet him; word's
got round as far as Australia.

MYLORD
2a Ickstattstraße, Tel: 2604498.
Daily, 5pm–1am; Saturday, 6pm–3am.
An institution in the Glockenbach
quarter.

TOGETHER
Hans-Sachs/Jahnstraße,
Tel: 263469.
Tuesday–Thursday 10.30pm–1am; Friday/Saturday, 10.30pm–3am.
Boy meets boy and girl meets girl.

Live Music

ALLOTRIA
3 Oskar-von-Miller-Ring, Tel: 285858.
Monday–Thursday 8.30pm–2am; Friday, Saturday till 3pm; Sunday 1–8pm.
Gerry Hayes' traditional bastion for
bebop, Dixie and big bands. Older
clientele—too expensive for the kids.

KAFFEE GIESING
5 Bergstraße, Tel: 6920579.
Daily, 10am–1am.
The owner, singer/songwriter, Konstantin Wecker, manages to stop the
place being taken over by the beautiful
people despite his success. Interesting
programme, original interior; what
could be better than a sunny Sunday
morning on the patio?

FEIERWERK
39 Hansastraße, Tel: 7693600.
Initiative started by social workers,
constantly on the brink of financial
ruin; worth seeing.

METROPOLIS
5 Bayerstraße, entrance Zweigstraße.
Tel: 598541/42.
Munich has been waiting for this centrally situated venue. Programme from
newspapers.

THEATERFABRIK UNTERFÖHRING
23 Föhringer Alle, Tel: 9504949.
Concert hall in the northern suburb of
Unterföhring: Jazz, Rock and Salsa.

UNTERFAHRT
96 Kirchenstraße, Tel: 4482794.
Daily, except Monday, 9pm–1am; Sunday from 10am.
Live music. The only 'pure' jazz pub
in Munich; a must for aficionados.

Shopping

What to Buy

What can you buy in Munich? Everything! *Where* you buy is a matter of personal taste. The whole city centre—from Odeonsplatz to Marienplatz, down to Tal and up to Stachus, Sendlingerstraße, Schelling/Türkenstraße, Leopoldstraße up from Franz-Joseph-Straße, Hohenzollernstraße from Leopoldstraße—contains the main shopping haunts. But it would only be half the fun if you knew precisely in advance where you could get what, and for how much. So here are the shops for essentials (also helpful services you can use when shopping).

Bavarian
Beer steins, blue-and-white and other checks can be found in the gift departments of all department stores plus the souvenir shops round the Viktualienmarkt. **Etcetera** in Würzerstraße has self-consciously witty Bavarica and other gifts.

Books
Book buying, one of my favourite occupations, is best done at **Hugendubel** on Marienplatz, as it has the biggest selection (also some English). However, masses of people shove through the 'book department store', so browsing isn't an unalloyed pleasure. The biggest English bookshop is **Anglia** (3 Schellingstraße), assuming the owner, on a higher intellectual plane, can find the book you want in the reigning chaos. See also **Words' Worth** (21a Schellingstraße).

If you long for foreign parts, **GEO Buchladen** (6 Rosental, on Viktualienmarkt) can provide you with everything about travel.

Find unusual examples of the comic as an art form at **Comic Company** (74

Baaderstraße). **Basis Buchhandlung** (41b Adalbertstraße, Tel: 2722828) has a large selection of reasonable second-hand/remaindered books. **Zweitausandeins** (65 Türkenstraße) has everything from its catalogue (alternative coffee table, unusual items) plus a large stock of records and cheap CDs.

Coiffure
Le Coup (Theatinerstraße/Odeonsplatz, Tel: 222327) will set your hair right for the evening. The Countess of Thurn and Taxis, notorious for her eccentric styles, is a regular customer! I hear that **Ulrich Graf** (10 Hans-Sachs-Straße, Tel: 2607067) is more unusual (for men and women both).

Contact Lenses/Glasses
Centrally situated for emergencies are: **Köck Optik** (Max-Weber-Platz, Tel: 471537) and **Söhnges Optik** (7 Brienner Straße, 34 Kaufinger Straße, Tel: 27290243).

Benny's Brillenstudio (Hans-Sachs-Straße 1, Tel: 269091) has a large selection of interesting styles from exclusive manufacturers.

Couture
Maximilianstraße: here designers like **Gucci** (No. 32), **Yves Saint Laurent** (No. 21), **Jil Sander** (No. 21), and Rudolph Moshammer's **Carneval de Venise** (No. 14) compete for the contents of ladies' *porte-monnaies*. On Theatinerstraße are **Rodier** (No. 29) and on Briennerstraße **Chanel** (No. 10) among other luminaries.

For men: **Max Dietl** (16 Residenzstraße), **Dunhill** (3 Maffeistraße), **L H van Hess** (3 Brienner Straße) and also **Hirmer** (22 Kaufingerstraße) and **Zechbauer** (13 Briennerstraße). If you've forgotten your tails or cutaway, **W Breuer** (22 Hohenzollernstraße) can save the day.

Jewellery
Diamonds are still a girl's best friend, in Munich as elsewhere. One of the city's best known jewellers is **Hemmerle** (14 Maximilianstraße). Another good bet is **Wempe** (10 Maximilianstraße, and 28 Kaufingerstraße). More reasonably priced jewellery, and a wide selection of pearls, is offered by **Mikado Perlen** (64 Sendlinger Straße, 6 Rindermarkt and 30 Färbergraben). **Cardiac** (27 Hohenzollernstraße) carries modern and handmade items.

Delicatessens
Where else but **Dallmayr** (14 Dienerstraße) or **Käfer** (73 Prinzregentenstraße) can you pamper your palate and your ego with delicacies? The Viktualienmarkt also has delicate foods next to the hearty stuff.

Invited out and want to take a present for your hosts?
Don't panic, for last minute purchases try **Glasmarkt** (30 Oberanger), **Glasmühle** (7 Sendlinger Straße) or **i-Düpferl** (37 Sendlinger Straße). Something to make a statement in designer apartments can be found at **Skrupel** (10 Herzogstraße). And **Porcelaine Blanche** (48 Schellingstraße) will supply you with everything in white.

Wines

Spanish: **Iberica** (49 Wörthstraße). French: **Jacques' Weindepot,** (199 Englschalkingerstraße), **Maison du Vin** (34 Hohenzollernstraße). Italian: **Garibaldi,** (60 Schellingstraße), **Giesinger Weinhandlung** (1 Hans-Mielich-Straße).

Flea markets

Many permanent flea market sites have fallen before Munich's busy bulldozers, and suitable alternatives are few and far between. The **Giesinger Trödelmarkt** in 26 Aschauerstraße has become popular after the fall of the Berlin Wall. Farmers' markets have also become a regular feature (Wednesday on Mariahilfplatz; Saturday, Fritz-Hommel-Weg near Nordfriedhof). An organic food market is at the corner of Türkenstraße/Theresienstraße).

Hats/Suitcases

Classy heads go to **Breiter** (23 Kaufingerstraße) and **Seidl** (6 Neuhauserstraße).

Need another suitcase to get all your loot home? **Baier** (7 Kaufingerstraße), **Münchner Werkstätten** (52 Karlstraße) or a branch of **Thalmessinger** (1 Theatinerstraße, 2 Karlsplatz) can help.

Left-handed

3 Brunnstraße/Asamhof—but nothing for people with two left feet.

Records, CDs

Beck on Marienplatz has a surprisingly good selection with its classical and jazz sections (fourth floor). And while you're here you'll certainly want to have a look at the fashion/décor and gift departments. The latter can usually supply the perfect last minute present.

Unusual records and CDs, with music from the four corners of the earth, can be found at **Shirokko** (19 Ledererstraße). **WOM World Of Music** (15 Kaufingerstraße) has the biggest and most comprehensive selection. You can listen to records over headphones, and pick up advance tickets in the foyer.

Cleaning

Fast stain removal: **Kingsgard** (130 Hohenzollernstraße), **Theresienreinigung** (31 Theresienstraße), **Wörth** (17 Rindermarkt/6 Münchener Freiheit).

Knick-knacks and secondhand

Leopoldmarkt (25 Leopoldstraße) has something more than the usual boutique/casual clothes store stuff—lots of accessories. Not bad are **Hallhuber,** on Marienplatz and 6 Hohenzollernstraße. If you don't mind a previous owner, **Lakumo** (13 Hans-Sachs-Straße, Monday–Friday, 11.30am– 6pm; Saturday, 11am–2pm) and **Zsa Zsa** (66 Schellingstraße) will deliver the goods.

Sport

Sport Scheck has the best selection (85 Sendlinger Straße), and it's a hive of activity, what with sheiks outfitting their offspring with the latest Puma/Adidas/Nike shoes. **Sport Schuster,** round the corner (3–6 Rosenstraße) is

sometimes cheaper. Secondhand clothes and gear are available at **Muskelkater** (19 Belgradstraße).

Traditional Costume

For fancy dressers: *Lederhosen* from **Moser** (Herzogspitalstraße) or **Wölfl** (20 Westenriederstraße), jackets (known as *Janker)* from **Loden-Frey** (7–9 Maffeistraße). And in Moosach, at 38 Triebstraße, **Loden** also has a discount shop.

Calendar of Special Events

Public Holidays

Fasching: Epiphany (6 January) to Ash Wednesday. For masked balls, near naked balls . . . get tickets in advance. High spots: **Bal Pare, Chrysanthemenball, Presseball, Große Glocke** of the *Abendzeitung* newspaper, **München Schabernackt, Weiße Feste** etc. The Munich gutter press run day-by-day reports. Every seven years, 1991 included, the **coopers** dance at the balls, an old custom dating from the Plague years. Every year, starting at dawn on Shrove Tuesday, the **market women dance** at the Viktualienmarkt—original costumes, and a 'real' Munich ritual.

Fairs and Festivals

Starkbierzeit—Strong Beer Weeks: third Friday after Ash Wednesday, for two weeks. Straight after Fasching the *-ator* beers arrive. What's in a name? Well, beware of *Animator, Delicator, Optimator, Triumphator* and *Salvator;* they guarantee neither triumph nor salvation—just a hangover. The latter was first brewed in 1630, by monks of

the Paulaner Monastery in the Au district, and every year at the barrel tapping ceremony, well-known political and other figures meet at the Salvatorkeller for general leg pulling.

ISPO: Spring and autumn. During the sports fair, hotels are full as far as Augsburg.

Frühlingsfest—Spring Fair: end of April. This mini-Oktoberfest takes place—usually in pouring rain—on the Theresienwiese. Its motto: we shall endure.

Caravan and Boat Fair: Crowds in spring and autumn flock to this travel fair, and the German imagination goes travelling.

Springfair: end of April, with a smaller beer festival on the Theresienwiese.

Auer Maidult—May Fair: Saturday before 1st May, for one week. *Dult* is Bavarian for fair or exhibition. Three times a year, in the shadow of the church at Mariahilfplatz, comes a mixture of antique market, junk sale and funfair. Old and new, cheap and exorbitant—you'll find it all at this eagerly awaited event.

Stadtgründungsfest: to mark the anniversary of the founding of the city, between Marienplatz and Odeonsplatz.

Filmfest München: end of June. An attempt to put Munich into competition with Berlin, Cannes, Venice etc on the world film circuit.

Floßfahrten—Raft Trips: this freshwater extravaganza is the Bavarian idea of fun: beer and oompah music the whole day, from Tölz to the Isar Canal in Munich, complete with sunburn, alcohol poisoning, and now and again a drowning.

Only whole rafts may be booked (carrying around 60 people), six to 12 months in advance (from, for example, Flößerei-Betriebe Seitner, Tel: 08171/18320). Watching is also fun, and your best vantage points are at Straßlach in the Mühltal valley.

Opernfestspiele—Opera Festival: July. Dinner jackets come out of mothballs for the annual laryngeal acrobatics. Order tickets well in advance if you want to hear the fat lady sing.

Jakobidult: Saturday after St James' Day, end of July.

Oktoberfest: Second-to-last Saturday in September, for two weeks. This internationally famous beer-fest is also known, locally as *Wies'n*. Innkeepers, the mayor, Bavarian VIPs and everybody else joins in the annual stein hoisting. **Saturday:** parade of the festival landlords, 12 noon; official tapping ceremony in Schottenhamel Tent. **Sunday:** 11am costume and riflemen's parade (Trachten-und-Schützenzug) through the whole town. See Option 12: *Oktoberfest* in the *Pick & Choose* section.

Modewoche—Fashion Week: Starts middle of August and lasts three days. Hotel rooms are hard to find, and scarcely a taxi or restaurant table free.

Kirchweihdult: third Saturday in October.

Antiquitätenmarkt—Antiques Market: end of October. This is the meeting place for restorers, dealers and polished-surface freaks.

Sechs-Tage-Rennen—Six-Day Race: November. This spectacle in the Olympiahalle is not so much about cycle racing as it is about low entertainment, beer and cheap thrills—loads of laughs if such things happen to turn you on.

Heim & Handwerk: end of November. This fair for do-it-yourselfers, plasterers and drillers is also open to the Great Unwashed.

Christkindlmärkte—Advent Markets: beginning the first Sunday in Advent. Crowds of people, mulled wine, Christmas tree decorations, bits and pieces and sausage stalls characterise the fair on Marienplatz. Things are quieter on Weißenburger Platz in Haidhausen. There are lovely arts and crafts, amateur and professional, at Münchener Freiheit; also live music, not only seasonal, a refreshing change from supermarket carols.

TRAVEL ESSENTIALS

When to Visit

The advantages of picking one season to visit Munich over another are simply matters of individual taste: the city's always got something to offer. However, I'd like to direct your attention towards early autumn. Not without good reason was the first Oktoberfest scheduled to fall in this season of guaranteed sun. The heat of high summer no longer scorches during the day, but the weather is still warm enough

for you to enjoy the bustle in the streets, one or two beers in a beer garden and the glorious Munich sunsets. 'Munich glows' is never more true than now. Many street cafés and beer gardens are especially attractive at this time of year, and at the start of the season there are hundreds of cultural activities and festivals. It's generally a good idea not to leave cardigans or pullovers at home, though, for the evening air can be cool.

Money Matters

Munich banks, with the exception of the banks at the Hauptbahnhof and the airport, open at the following times: Monday to Friday, 8.30/9am–12.30/1pm and 1.45/2–3.30pm; Thursday open till 5.30/6pm.

Hauptbahnhof: daily, 6am–11.30pm.

Most banks pay out cash for credit cards. There are plenty of cash machines.

Driving in the City

A warning: Munich is about to suffocate in traffic, and finding a parking space in the city centre is like winning the lottery. Leave your car where you're staying or outside town, and use the excellent system of public transport, take a taxi or walk.

All the motorways listed below (except Munich West) come out on the Middle Ring Road (Mittlerer Ring). Mornings and evenings, often as late as 8pm for no apparent reason, you'll find traffic jams on these three-lane 'cityways'. Follow the signs to the Nürnberg motorway (Autobahn) and you'll end up in the north of Munich; the Salzburg motorway, in the southeast; the Garmisch motorway, in the south; the Lindau motorway, in the southwest; and the Stuttgart motorway, in the west. Before the end of each motorway there are officials who can provide you with information and help. If you're planning a day trip to Munich and coming via the outlying villages/inter-city roads, use the 'Park and Ride' system and leave your car at the U-Bahn terminuses.

A9: Berlin/Würzburg–Nürnberg–Ingolstadt–Munich–Schwabing.

A94: Passau–Munich–Riem–Munich–Steinhausen.

A8: Salzburg–Rosenheim–Munich–Ramersdorf (officials' station, Tel: 089/672555).

E995: Salzburg–Rosenheim–Munich–Giesing.

A95: Garmisch–Munich–Kreuzhof.

A96: Lindau–Landsberg am Lech–Munich–Sendling.

A8: Stuttgart-ulm-Munich-West (officials' station, Tel: 089/8112412).

Munich Motorway Service: Fasagartenstraße 73, 8000 München 83, Tel: 089/672099.

Two car parks, in case you can't do without: at **Stachus** (entrance via Sonnen/Bayerstraße). Monday to Friday 7am–midnight, Sunday and holidays 1pm–midnight. At **Färbergraben** (entrance via Herzogspitalstraße). Monday to Friday, 7am—midnight; Sunday and holidays closed.

At the Station

The newly renovated terminus station in post-Modernist design, with a wide choice of hotels in the vicinity, is not far from Stachus and the pedestrian zone and has very good S-Bahn (suburban rail), bus, U-Bahn (underground), tram and taxi connections.

The German Railways information centre (DB-Reisezentrum) has all the important information, timetables etc you'll need. The 'city within the city' in the station has everything a traveller could desire, including an enormous range of books, magazines and newspapers from all over the world.

The Bayerstraße exit (by the low platform numbers) leads to the south and west, the Arnulfstraße exit (high platform numbers) to the north and east of Munich.

At the Airport

Riem Airport was superseded in 1992 by the major new Franz Josef Strauß airport at Erding. The terminal has been designed to cater for 15 million air travellers and is divided into 4 modules. Module A: Lufthansa inland flights. Module B: Lufthansa flights abroad. Module C: intercontinental and non-EC flights of other airlines. Module D: EC-flights.

Air transfer: Travel on the motorways A9 and A89 to the centre usually takes 40 minutes, but during rush-hour these routes are prone to delays. The S8 takes 40 minutes between the airport and the Hauptbahnhof and has specially designed blue carriages. A taxi to the Hauptbahnhof costs around DM70. There is also a bus shuttle service to the Hauptbahnhof.

MINI-GUIDE TO THE CITY

Geography and Topography

The city of Munich has a total area of 310km^2 (around 120 square miles), and is 117km (73 miles) in circumference. The geographical centre (north of the Cathedral towers) has a latitude of 48° 8' 23" north and longitude of 11° 34' 28" east.

The average height above sea level is 530m (1,740ft), rising to just under 580m above sea level (1,905ft) at its highest point. At the time of writing Munich has 1.263 million inhabitants (figures from 31 December 1988).

The Weather and its Effects

As you would expect from Munich's location—only 50km (31 miles) from the Alps—and from its height, the climate is more extreme than in more northerly regions while seeming to be better than in the rest of Germany. The reason for this is the *Föhn* (approximate pronunciation: 'fern'), which looks like fine weather to tourists, but which gives Munich residents headaches and increases their bloody-mindedness. An autumn wind sweeping down from the Alps and warming up quickly, the *Föhn* brings bright blue skies, small white clouds and a perfectly clear view, which can be seen to its best advantage from the following high points:

Frauenturm (Cathedral tower), 98m (322ft), April–October: Monday–Saturday, 10am–5pm; closed Sunday and holidays; DM4.
Alter Peter (Old St Peter's), 92m (302ft): Monday–Saturday, 9am–6pm; Sunday and holidays, 10am–6pm (depending on weather); DM2.
Rathausturm (Town Hall Tower), 85m:

Monday–Friday, 9am–4pm; weekends and holidays, closed; DM2.
Olympiaturm (Olympic Tower), 290m (951ft): daily, 9am–midnight (last trip up 11.30pm); DM4.

Munich and Foreigners

To the great displeasure of many a bad tempered native clad in Loden green, you just can't drink a beer on your own here any more. *They* flood in from all corners of the globe, these tourists, breaching the royal Bavarian peace in the (mega-) village. And it's not only the foreigners—the blow-ins clutter up this lovely city as well, spending their ill-gotten gains on loose living. The fear of the colonized race sometimes finds expression in the rough but picturesque formulation 'They're all bloody Prussians'—a turn of phrase which recurs with regularity. Those addressed in this way take it with equanimity. After all, it doesn't mean they're North Germans, not by a long shot; there are Japanese and African Prussians too!

TOURIST INFORMATION

Tourist Information Office

First aid for the lost and bewildered can be found in the small yellow programme put out by the Tourist Information Office: *Offizielles Monatsprogramm des Fremdenverkehrsamtes*. This contains details of events, useful addresses and a list of hotels and pensions. You can get it for DM1.80 at any newspaper stand or shop. Munich Tourist Information Office (Fremdenverkehrsamt München) will answer enquiries in writing: Postfach, 8000 München 1. Or over the phone: Tel: 089/23911 (main switchboard)—if somebody answers.

Information on Accommodation

Fremdenverkehrsverband München/ Oberbayern eV (Munich and Upper Bavaria Tourist Information).

0 Sonnenstraße/Third floor, 8000 Munich 2. Tel: 089/597347

Hauptbahnhof (Bayerstraße exit). Tel: 089/2391–256 or 257. Daily, 8am–11pm. No room reservations by phone.

Rindermarkt/Pettenbeckstraße. Tel: 089/2391272. Monday–Friday, 9.30am–6pm.

Rathaus (Turmzimmer im Prunkhof): Town Hall, Tower Room in courtyard Monday–Friday, 9am–5pm, closed weekends and public holidays.

Stadtinformation (City Information Office) in Karlsplatz Stachus Lower Level.
Monday–Friday, 8am–6pm, closed weekends and public holidays. Tel: 089/554459—someone usually answers.

Museums, galleries: Tel: 089/2391–61.
Castles, sights: Tel: 089/2391–71.

AROUND TOWN

Maps

Street maps and others (maps for cyclists or walkers, S-Bahn maps etc) can be bought at kiosks and bookshops. The best for a short stay in Munich is a map of the main city with the sights and sites marked on it.

City Tours

The most comfortable way to get acquainted with Munich is via a bus tour. City tours start diagonally across from the main entrance to the Hauptbahnhof (corner of Schützenstraße):

Short Tour:
Daily, 10am and 2.30pm; DM13, 1hr.

Extended Short Tour:
Daily, 10am and 2.30pm; DM20, around 2hrs 30mins.

Long Tour:
Daily except Monday, 10am (includes Cathedral/Alte Pinakothek); DM23, around 2hrs 30mins.
Daily except Monday, 2.30pm (includes Nymphenburg Palace); DM23, around

2hrs 30mins.
On public holidays please check by calling 089/1204248.

Public Transport

The S-Bahn doors frozen shut—or open—in winter, four buses arriving at one-minute intervals and then a 15-minute wait for the next, and the incomprehensible Bavarian announcements—don't let all this put you off using the otherwise excellent system as much as possible.

The most typical of all the methods of transport is the tram. Unfortunately, the days of the trams are numbered, for technical and economic reasons.

Second place goes to the U-Bahn (underground), the fastest way of getting around Munich. It's a direct offspring of Munich's rise in status to Olympic City in 1972, and has been extended constantly since then.

The S-Bahn (surface railway/rapid transit) lines serve thousands of commuters within a 40km (25 mile) radius every day. Because of this, they're cheek-to-jowl full in the rush hour.

The blue-and-white Munich buses face a serious problem: there are no bus-only lanes in Munich. Thus, buses finish last in the Munich Public Transport Authority race.

Tickets and Rules

If you're in Munich for a short stay, it's cheapest to buy strip or daily tickets from the machines or at kiosks. On the machines are lists of destinations and the appropriate number of strips you have to cancel (that is, stamp). Note that the stamping machines are not in the U- and S-Bahn carriages, but only on the platforms or at station entrances. You can change trains, etc as often as you like and travel for up to one hour within a given zone; a single ticket is valid for all methods of transport. However, you must not change direction. That counts as faredodging (*Schwarzfahren*—literally, 'travelling black'), and carries a fine of DM60.

Short journeys require one strip. The inner (first) zone reqires two strips and each further zone a further two strips, up to a maximum of 10 strips for five zones and upward.

On buses and trams a short journey is four stops; on U- and S-Bahns, 2 stops.

Children need one strip of the children's strip ticket for up to two zones; three zones or more, two strips.

Einzelfahrtkarte (single ticket) for journeys of short distance: DM1.30, 1 zone: DM2.50.

Streifenkarte (large) 10 strips: DM10.

Day ticket—inner zone: adults: DM7.50, children: DM2.50.

Day ticket—outer zone: adults: DM8, children: DM8.

Day ticket—all zones: adults: DM16, children: DM4.50.

Bicycles can be taken on U- and S-Bahn trains at the following times (at

the time of writing, three strips are needed): Monday–Friday, 8.30am–3 pm, and 6.30pm–close of service. Saturday, Sunday and public holidays, the whole day. More information from: **Münchner Verkehrs- und Tarifverbund.** 2 Thierschstraße, 8000 Munich 22. Tel: 2191-3322.

Taxis

Munich taxi drivers are a breed unto themselves. No one really knows exactly who they are, except that at night they're all students and by day they're all 'pros'. A typical Munich taxi driver is proud of knowing the city like the back of his hand, so don't try to tell him which route to take or you could end up walking there. Most drivers adhere to the rule of 'the shortest route', a rarity in the world today. In fact, Munich drivers are classed as comparatively benign altogether.

The basic tariff is DM3.90 at press time, plus DM2.20 for every kilometre travelled. An additional charge of DM1 is made on telephone bookings, also for every suitcase and animal(!). An hour of waiting time costs DM24. The whole area of the MVV is now covered by taxi services.

Advance bookings: Tel: 21610, 19410.

Deliveries and errands: Tel: 216157, 264220.

You can find out the location of he nearest taxi rank by consulting the inside cover of the telephone book.

By Bicycle

The city so famous for its fancy cars and scarcity of parking spaces has recently begun to plan more cycle paths and take more notice of people parking across existing ones. Munich really is developing into a city of cyclists. Their numbers have increased so much that reports of collisions with other road users have escalated and turn many a cyclist's and pedestrian's soul white-hot with rage. Despite this, cycling in Munich is still a pleasure, above all because of the English Garden and the miles of cycle paths along the Isar. Even if you're only in Munich for a short while, you should take advantage of this and hire a bike. If you're on foot, keep your eyes peeled for cycling speed demons.

Bicycles are allowed on public transport at certain times (see above). You'll find tips for bike tours in a leaflet obtainable from the Tourist Information Office.

ADFC (Allgemeiner Deutscher Fahrrad

Club; German Cycle Association). 17 Steinstraße. Tel: 089/4801001. One of Munich's major pressure groups. They supply you with all you need to know about cycles.

A-Z Fahrräder, 8 Zweibrückenstraße. Tel: 223272.

Transpedal (courier service). 24 Alramstraße, M70. Tel: 779033; Monday–Friday, 8am–6pm.

Fahrradverleih am Englischen Garten (cycle hire). Dr Martin Buss, Office: 1 Habsburger Platz. Tel: 089/397016; Monday–Saturday, 10am–6 pm (summer only).

Lothar Borucki. 7 Hans-Sachs-Straße, M5. Tel: 266506; Monday–Friday, 9am–1pm and 3–6pm; Saturday, 9am–noon.

Radl-R. 8 Kurfürstenstraße (courtyard), M40. Tel: 349110.

On Foot
In Munich, as in every city, the maxim 'discretion is the better part of valour' applies. Caution is the cardinal virtue on pavements and roads. *Homo erectus* can accomplish practically everything on foot in Munich, at least in the centre. Another request: please don't set children a bad example by crossing roads when the pedestrian light is red as the accident statistics are far too high already.

WHERE TO STAY

Hotels and Pensions
Munich boasts the most-visited hotels in Germany, even if the Guild of Hoteliers thinks otherwise. It's wise to book well in advance, especially if you plan to come at the time of the Oktoberfest or the big trade fairs. And if you want to come when a trade fair's on, you may well have to put up with increased prices.

There are fewer and fewer lower and middle-class hotels in the city, while luxury and upper-class hotels are springing up like mushrooms. The choice we offer here includes four categories and gives the price of a double room with breakfast. These prices can be used as a rule of thumb for single rooms, whose prices are usually not much lower.

Luxury Class
Bayerischer Hof and Palais Montgelas. 2–6 Promenadenplatz, M2. Tel: 089/21200. Double DM399–519.
Exclusive grand hotel, famous for nightclub and Trader Vic's.

Continental Royal, Classic Hotel. 5 Max-Joseph-Straße, M2. Tel: 089/551570. Double DM320–500.
Hotel in the finest traditions of elegance, with exquisite interior.

City Hilton. 15 Rosenheimerstraße. Tel: 089/4804–0. Double DM327–447. Luxury hotel on the English Garden.

Hilton Park. Am Tucherpark, M22. Tel: 089/3845–0. Double DM409–556. Luxury hotel on the English Garden.

Königshof. Karlsplatz (Stachus), M2. Tel: 089/551360. Double DM365–494. Elegant luxury hotel in the centre.

Palace Hotel. 21 Trogerstraße, M80. Tel: 4705091. Double DM337–494. Small, extremely elegant hotel in Bogenhausen, with every convenience.

Sheraton Hotel. 6 Arabellastraße, M81. Tel: 089/9264–0. Double DM374–404. The largest top-class hotel in Munich.

Vier Jahreszeiten Kempinski München. 17 Maximilianstraße, M2. Tel:

089/230390. Double DM548–628.
Classy establishment at the opera (probably the best hotel in Munich).

125 to 515 DM

An der Oper. 10 Falkenturmstraße, M2. Tel: 089/290027–0. Double DM193–215.
Small hotel, often hosting distinguished operatic guests.

Consul. 10 Viktoriastraße. Tel: 089/334035-37. Double DM160–180.
Nice hotel in Schwabing.

Penta Hotel. 3 Hochstraße, M80. Tel: 089/4485555. Double DM322–392.
Large hotel with excellent facilities, opposite Gasteig Cultural Centre. Airline hotel.

Preysing. 1 Preysingstraße, M80. Tel: 089/481011. Double DM284–515.
Elegant hotel with faultless service and cuisine in the Preysing-Keller.

Residence. 4 Artur-Kutscher-Platz, M40. Tel: 089/38178–0. Double DM248–350.
In a quiet part of Schwabing.

Splendid. 54 Maximilianstraße, M22 Tel: 089/296606. Double DM125–325.
Small hotel at the Max II Monument.

66 to 185 DM

Am Markt. 6 Heiliggeiststraße, M2. Tel: 089/226844. Double DM98–140.
Bavarian, cosy, very quiet, directly on the Viktualienmarkt.

Blauer Bock. 16 Blumenstraße, M2.

Tel: 089/2608043. Double DM85–145
Simple, good location at the Viktu alienmarkt.

Englischer Garten. 8 Liebergesell straße, M40. Tel: 089/393034–6. Dou ble DM127–172.
Small hotel, excellent location.

Leopold. 117 Leopoldstraße, M40. Tel 089/367081. Double DM95–185.
Small hotel, but good address in the north of Schwabing.

Lettl. 53 Amalienstraße, M40. Tel 089/283026. Double DM165–210.
Near the university; guests and atmosphere to match the location.

Mariandl. 51 Goethestraße, M2. Tel: 089/534108. Double DM90–120.
Restaurant with live classical music.

Olympic garni. 4 Hans-Sachs-Straße, M5. Tel: 089/23189–0. Double DM165–240.
Small but comfortable hotel in the Glockenbach district.

Präsident. 13 Lindwurmstraße. Tel: 089/263011. Double DM99–210.
Not far from Sendlinger Tor.

Stephanie garni. 35 Türkenstraße, M40. Tel: 089/284031–3. Double DM110–140.
Distinguished, adjacent the major art museums in Schwabing.

Theresia. 51 Luisenstraße, M2. Tel: 089/521250, 5233081. Double DM66–105. Simple, close to the Pinakotheken.

Uhland. 1 Uhlandstraße. Tel: 089/539277. Double DM130–220.
Quiet hotel near the Theresienwiese.

Camping

München-Thalkirchen. 49 Zentralländerstraße. Tel: 089/7231707. Open mid-March to the end of October.

München-Obermenzing. At the start of the Stuttgart motorway. Tel:

89/8112235. Open mid-March to the beginning of November.

Further information.

Accommodation for young people
Youth Hostel (Jugendherberge). 20 Wendl-Dietrich-Straße, M19. Tel: 089/131156.

Jugendherberge Burg Schwaneck. Pullach, Munich. Tel: 089/7930643.

Haus International, young people's guest house. 87 Elisabethstraße, M40. Tel: 089/120060.

OPENING TIMES

Munich shops usually open from 9am–6.30pm. Some design or fashion shops don't open until 10 or even 11am. Generally it's only the smaller shops which take a midday break. Since the autumn of 1989, the city centre shops at least have stayed open until 8 or even 8.30pm on Thursday. On the first Saturday of the month, almost all shops except supermarkets and food shops stay open till 4pm.

PUBLIC HOLIDAYS

We give only those holidays which may fall on a weekday:

New Year	1 January
Epiphany	6 January
Shrove Tuesday	
Good Friday	
Easter Monday	
May Holiday	1 May
Ascension Day	
Whit Monday	
Corpus Christi	
The Assumption	15 August
German Unification Day	
	3 October
All Souls' Day	1 November
Day of Prayer and Repentance	
Christmas Day	25 December
Boxing Day	26 December

HEALTH & EMERGENCIES

Emergency Telephone Numbers

Police. Tel: 110.

Fire Brigade. Tel: 112.

Ambulance. Tel: 19222.

Emergency Medical Attention (National Health). Tel: 558661.

Emergency Chemist. Tel: 594475.

Emergency Telephone Service for Addicts. Tel: 282822.

Alcoholics' Advisory Service. Tel: 5207-342/351/428/393.

Samaritans. Tel: 11101 (Protestant); Tel: 11102 (Catholic).

Chemists and Clinics

Bahnhof-Apotheke (international). 2 Bahnhofplatz. Tel: 089/594119.

Europaapotheke (international). 12 Schützenstraße. Tel: 089/595423.

Internationale Ludwigsapotheke. 8 Neuhauser Straße. Tel: 089/2608011.

Universitätspoliklinik (University Outpatients' Clinic). 8a Pettenkoferstraße. Tel: 089/5160–0.

Frauenklinik der Universität (University Women's Clinic). 11 Maistraße. Tel: 089/5160–0.

Kinderklinik der Universität (University Pediatric Clinic). 4 Lindwurmstraße. Tel: 089/5160–0.

Zahnklinik der Universität (University Dental Clinic). 70 Goethestraße. Tel: 089/5160-0.

Augenklinik der Universität (University Opthalmological Clinic). 8 Mathildenstraße. Tel: 089/5160-0.

Breakdowns

ADAC-Stadtpannendienst—German Automobile Association. City Breakdown Service. Tel: 089/19211.

ACE-Pannendienst—Auto Club Europe Breakdown Service. Tel: 089/19216.

DTC-Pannendienst—Deutscher Touring Automobil Club Breakdown Service. Tel: 089/8111212.

Lost Property Offices

City Administration Lost Property Office (property lost on the street and in public transport). 19 Ruppertstraße, M2. Tel: 089/233-1. Monday–Friday 8.30am–noon; Tuesday, also 2.30–5.30pm; closed weekends and holidays.
Fundstelle der Bundesbahn (Lost Property Office of the German Federal Railways). 2 Hauptbahnhof-Bahnhofplatz (opposite Platform 26). Tel: 089/1286664. Daily, 6.30am–11.30pm. 472 Landbergerstraße. Tel: 089/1285859. Monday–Friday 8am–noon, Thursday 12.30–3pm.

Ostbahnhof Lost Property Office. (property lost on S-Bahns—except S6 line). Tel: 089/12884409. Monday–Friday, 8am–5.45 pm; Saturday 8am–11.45am. Closed Sunday and holidays.

Publications

For English-only-speakers, *Munich Sounds* is available at the central station or the Anglia book shop (3 Schellingstraße). The flagship of Munich's media is undoubtedly the *Süddeutsche Zeitung,* undisputedly the best both in terms of circulation and the quality of its journalism. Vital for anyone new to Munich: its large sections of advertisements of jobs and flats. Important for tourists: its daily listings of events, especially on Friday.

One of the few popular papers to enjoy a following among the more intellectual is the *Abendzeitung (AZ).* This is primarily due to its arts and cultural review section and to Ponkie, its linguistic acrobat. The *tageszeitung (tz)* is also in the popular press stable and comes from the same publishers as the conservative *Münchner Merkur.*

Daily theatre, cinema, concerts, television and radio details may be found in all papers, which may be bought at kiosks, from special machines (you need the correct change!) and from paper sellers on the streets and in pubs and restaurants.

Disciples of the cult of the Modern Age go for the monthly magazine *Prinz;* alternative tendencies prefer the bi-weekly *Münchner Stadtmagazin.* The programme listings magazine, *in München,* also falls into the category 'contemporary', although it doesn't have a great number of articles. It's distributed free every second Thursday to some pubs and all cinemas for your edification and entertainment.'Serious' higher level culture (theatres and galleries in particular) is catered for by

Applaus and *München Mosaik* (both monthlies). And for all you swingers and boppers out there, may I recommend the monthly *Jazz-Zeitung*.

If your hobby is hunting things down, the small ads publication *Kurz und Fündig* will help you find whatever you're looking for.

Television and Radio

Munich television watchers, voluntarily and involuntarily armed with cable TV, now have a choice of around 20 channels, most of a quality leaving something to be desired. The two Austrian channels are really good (also English programmes in dual-language broadcast or with subtitles).

'A rich simplicity' is also a fitting description of the private radio stations; Radio Xanadu (93.30MHz) is a lively exception.

'Classical around the clock' in strange combinations can be heard on the Fourth Programme of the Bayerischer Rundfunk, Bavarian Radio (93.19MHz). Their First Programme is full of folksy yodellers (93.70MHz). Bayern 2 (92.20MHz) is on a higher intellectual plane. If you listen to Bayern 3 (92.55MHz), you get the impression the whole world is one gigantic traffic jam. The other stations differ only in their signature tunes.

Post and Telecommunications

Post offices (Postamt) in Munich usually open from 8am–6pm; Saturdays, from 8am–noon.

Post Office No. 32 (the Telegraph Office opposite the Hauptbahnhof main entrance) is always open. Public telex and telefax office: open daily, from 7am–11pm. There is also a *poste restaurante* office. The Post Office Savings Bank, cheque payment office and bureau de change are also open at night. Public script-display telephone for the deaf. Parcels and registered consignments not accepted.

To dial other countries first dial the international access code 00, then the relevant country code as follows: Australia (61); France (33); Italy (39); Japan (81); Netherlands (31); Spain (34); UK (44); US and Canada (1). If you are using a US credit phone card, you must first dial the company's access number as given below – Sprint, Tel: 0130 0013; AT&T, Tel: 0130 0010; MCI, Tel: 0130 0012.

SPECIAL TIPS

Children and Young People

Looking for a flat in Munich if you have a child/children is like running the gauntlet—and that's before you have to start paying the rent.

However—or *for* this reason—Munich provides or finances a whole range of activities for children and young people, either alone or with their parents. Let's start at the (baby's) bottom:

Babysitting Service. Tel: 089/2292911.

Kinderkino (Children's Cinema) in Gasteig. 5 Rosenheimer Straße . Tel: 089/48098–0.

Münchner Theater für Kinder—Children's Theatre. 46 Dachauer Straße, M2. Tel: 089/595454 or 593858.

Das Münchner Marionettentheater. 29a Blumenstraße, M2. Tel: 089/ 265712.

Die Münchner Puppenspiele im Münchner Stadtmuseum—marionette plays in the Municipal Museum. 1 Sankt-Jakobs-Platz, M2. Tel: 089/ 2314150.

Otto Bille's Marionettenbühne in Ludwig Krafft Theater. 15 Bereitanger/ corner of Zeppelinstraße, M90. Tel: 089/1502186 or 3101278.

Zirkus Krone. 43 Marsstraße, M2. Tel: 089/558168.

Hellabrunn Zoo. 6 Siebenbrunner, M90. Daily 8am–6pm (in winter 9am–5pm).

Theater der Jugend (Young People's Theatre). 47 Franz-Joseph-Straße, M40. Tel: 089/23721365.

JIZ Jugendinformationszentrum (Young People's Information Centre). 22 Paul-Heyse-Straße, M2. Tel: 089/51410660.

Women

Giesinger Frauentreff. 1 St-Martin Straße.

Frauenbuchladen. 57 Arcisstraße. Tel: 089/2721205.

Frauenkulturhaus. 21 Richard-Strauss-Straße. Tel: 089/4705212.

Mädchenpower-Café. 16 Baldestraße. Tel: 089/2026363.

Further addresses can be found in the *Nightlife* Section.

The Handicapped

There is an excellent directory obtainable from the City Information Office at Stachus, Lower Level.

Gay/Lesbian

The Munich gay scene meets around Glockenbach and Gärtnerplatz.

Subzentrum Schwuler Männer. 38 Müllerstraße. Tel: 089/2603056.

Szenenrand. 31 Auenstraße.

Lesbentelefon (lesbian line). Tel: 089/7254272. Friday, 6–10pm.

Lesbencafe. 3 Güllstraße, M2 (Women's Therapy Centre).

SPORT

Participant

Jogging is as *in* as ever. Whether you're a student, manager or hair stylist, Munich requires you to make an effort to be fit. This kind of sport is easiest to go about in the parks and gardens. Just have a look at a street map to find out where suitable places are— they're often extensive enough for marathon running too.

For all sport enthusiasts, active or passive, in the **Städtisches Sportamt**— City Sports Office, 26 Neuhauser Straße. Tel: 089/2338752, you'll find a brochure called *Sport und Spiel in München (Sport and Games in Munich)* telling you all your sports fan's heart (lungs etc) might want to know.

Information about **climbing** from **Deutscher Alpenverein** (German Alpine Society), 5 Praterinsel. Tel: 089/235090.

And if you're a **riding** fan, you can get a leg up from **Bayerischer Reit und Fahrverband** (Bavarian Riding and Driving Association), 11 Landshamer Straße. Tel: 089/906071.

Skating regardless of the season **Eissportstadion im Olympiapark**, Spiridon-Louis-Ring. Tel: 089/30613235. Check prices/opening times by phone.

Art nouveau adds a whole new dimension to **swimming** and sweating at the **Müllersches Volksbad** (Bath House), 1 Rosenheimer Straße. Tel: 089/2338946. Check prices/opening times by phone. You can also get an information brochure about other pools and baths in Munich.

Sailors seek guidance from **Bayerischer Segler-Verband** (Bavarian Sailing Association), 93 Georg-Bräuchle-Ring, M50. Tel: 089/ 1574672.

You can find **tennis** courts to hire by the hour all over Munich, especially at the Sport Scheck chain (Yellow Pages).

Spectator

Football: national league and European Cup, FC Bayern München, 51 Säbener Straße. Tel: 089/69931–0. Football: Bavarian League with local colour. 1860 München eV, 114 Grünwalder Straße. Tel: 089/643048.

Advance ticket sales: Veranstaltungsdienst Olympiapark, Im Eissportstadion. Tel: 089/30613577.

Horses and jockeys whizzing past at weekends: Münchner Rennverein eV, 36 Graf-Lehndorff-Straße. Tel: 089/ 908881.

The Gesundheitspark ('Health Park') Spiridon-Louis-Ring (under the western curve of the Olympic Stadium, Tel: 089/306101–0), offers a range of sporting, psychological and creative events.

USEFUL ADDRESSES

Banks

Bank für Gemeinwirtschaft.
8 Promenadenplatz, M2.
Tel: 089/21000.

Bayerische Hypotheken-und Wechsel-Bank.
9–17 Theatinerstraße, M2.
Tel: 089/92440.

Bayerische Vereinsbank.

14 Kardinal-Faulhaber-Straße, M2.
Tel: 089/21321.

Commerzbank.
21 Maximiliansplatz, M2.
Tel: 089/21961.

Deutsche Bank AG.
15 Promenadenplatz, M2.
Tel: 089/23900.

Dresdner Bank AG.
15 Promenadenplatz, M2.
Tel: 089/21390.

Postgiroamt.
26 Sonnenstraße, M2.
Tel: 089/51230.
Monday–Thursday, 8.30am–3pm. Friday till 2.30pm.

Stadtsparkasse München.
1 Thomas-Wimmer-Ring, M2.
Tel: 089/21670.

Airlines

Air France.
23 Theatinerstraße.
Tel: 089/21067.

Austrian Airlines.
9 Promenadenplatz.
Tel: 089/226666.

Iberia.
16 Schwanthalerstraße.
Tel: 089/558491.

KLM Royal Dutch Airlines.
37 Sendlinger Straße.
Tel: 089/268026.

Lufthansa.
1 Lenbachplatz. Tel: 089/51130.

SAS Scandinavian Airlines.
Riem Airport.
Tel: 089/908021.

Swissair.
21 Marienplatz.
Tel: 089/23633.

See also the Yellow Pages under *Luftverkehr* (Air Traffic).

Car Hire
In the Yellow Pages you'll find a wide range of car hire firms. Take advantage of the cheap weekend rates and compare prices—there are big differences.
A selection:

Fahr & Spar.
Tel: 089/508233.

Autohansa.
Tel: 089/504068.

Hertz.
Tel: 089/01302121.

Sixt Budget.
Tel: 089/223333.

Sport Car Rent.
Tel: 089/334400.

Travel Agencies
Amtliches Bayerisches Reisebüro.
Switchboard for all branches: Tel: 089/12040.

Autobus Oberbayern GmbH.
1 Lenbachplatz and other branches.
Tel: 089/558061.

Hapag-Lloyd-Reisebüro.
32 Theatinerstraße/First floor and other branches.
Tel: 089/5151–0.

Wagons-Lits.
3 Lenbachplatz and other branches.
Tel: 089/591167.

CULTURAL AFFAIRS

Museums
See also Tour 7: *An Afternoon of Art.* Phone to check times of opening hours on public holidays.

Alte Pinakothek.
27 Barer Straße (North Entrance).
Tel: 089/23805215.
Daily except Monday, 9.15am–4.30pm; Tuesday and Thursday, also 7.15–9pm.

Antikensammlungen (Collection of Antiquities).
1 Königsplatz.
Tel: 089/598359.
Tuesday and Thursday–Sunday, 10am–4.30pm; Wednesday noon–8.30pm.

Bayerisches Nationalmuseum (Collection of German historical art and folklore).
3 Prinzregentenstraße.
Tel: 089/2168–0.
Daily except Monday, 9.30am–5pm.

BMW Museum.
130 Petuelring.
Tel: 089/38953307.
Daily, 9am–5pm (last admission, 4.15pm).

Deutsches Jagd- und Fischereimuseum (Hunting and Fishing Museum).
53 Neuhauser Straße.
Tel: 089/220522.
Daily except Monday, 9.30am–5pm; Monday and Thursday, 9.30–9pm.

Deutsches Museum.
Ludwigsbrücke Bridge.
Tel: 089/21791.
Daily, 9am-5pm.

Deutsches Theatermuseum.
4a Galeriestraße (Hofgarten).
Tel: 089/222449.
Tuesday, 10am–noon, and Thursday, 2–4pm.
No permanent exhibits.

Erstes Nachttopfmuseum der Welt (World's First Chamber Pot Museum) (I'm not having you on).
30 Böcklinstraße.
Tel: 089/1575989.
Thursday, 2–6pm, Sunday, 10am–1pm.

Glyptothek.
3 Königsplatz.
Tel: 089/7286100.
Daily except Monday, 10am–4.30pm; Thursday, noon–8.30pm.

Jüdisches Museum München (Munich Jewish Museum).
36 Maximilianstraße.
Tel: 089/297453.
Tuesday and Wednesday, 2–6pm; Thursday, 2–9pm.

Historisches Nähmaschinen-Museum (Sewing-Machine Museum).
68–70 Heimeranstraße.
Tel: 089/510880.
Sewing-Machine Museum, weekdays, 10am–4pm. Ironing Museum, only on request.

KZ-Gedenkstätte Dachau (Dachau Concentration Camp Museum).
Tel: 081/311741.
Daily except Monday, 9am–5pm.

Münchner Puppenmuseum (Munich Doll Museum).
37 Gondershauser Straße.
Tel: 089/328950.
Monday and Thursday, 11am–5pm. Sunday, 10am–1pm, or by arrangement.

Münchner Stadtmuseum (Munich Municipal Museum).
Morris Dancers exhibit, armoury, brewing museum, photography museum, musical instrument collection, mari-

onette museum, film museum (programme 089/2335586).
1 St-Jakobs-Platz, 8000, м2.
Tel: 089/23323370.
Daily except Monday, 9.15am–5pm; Wednesday, 10am–8.30pm.

Neue Pinakothek.
29 Barerstraße (entrance on Theresienstraße).
Tel: 089/238050.
Daily except Monday, 9am–4.30pm; Tuesday, also 7–9pm.

Die Neue Sammlung (Artefacts and Design Museum).
3 Prinzregentenstraße.
Tel: 089/227844.
Open to the public only for special exhibitions.

Palaeontological Museum.
10 Richard-Wagner-Straße.
Tel: 089/5203361.
Monday–Thursday, 8am–4pm; Friday, 8am–3pm. Film show on the first Sunday of the month.

State Prehistoric Collection.
2 Lerchenfeldstraße.
Tel: 089/7293911.
Tuesday–Sunday, 9am–4pm; Thursday, 9am–8pm.

Residence Museum.
3 Max-Joseph-platz.
Tel: 089/290671.
Tuesday–Sunday, 10am–4.30pm.

Schack Gallery.
9 Prinzregentenstraße.
Tel: 089/23805224.
Daily except Tuesday, 9am–4.30pm.

Siemens Museum.
10 Prannerstraße. Tel: 089/2342660.
Monday–Friday, 9am–4pm; Saturday/Sunday, 10am–2pm.

Der Silbersalon im Alten Hackerhaus (Silver Salon).
75 Sendlinger Straße, Second floor (entrance in Hackerstraße).
Saturday, 1–5pm; Sunday, 10am–5pm.

Spielzeugmuseum (Toy Museum).
Old Town Hall.
Marienplatz.
Tel: 089/294001.
Monday–Saturday, 10am–5.30pm; Sunday and holidays, 10am–6pm.

State Collection of Graphic Art.
Study Room,10 Meiserstraße.
Tel: 089/5591490.
Monday–Thursday, 10am–1pm; Monday–Wednesday, also 2–4.30pm; Thursday, 2–6pm; Friday 10am-12.30pm.

Staatliche Münzsammlung (State Coinage Collection).
1 Residenzstraße. Tel: 089/227221.
Daily except Monday, 10am–4.30pm.

State Collection of Egyptian Art.
1 Hofgartenstraße (at the obelisk).
Tel: 089/298546.
Tuesday–Friday 9am–4pm; Tuesday 7–9pm; Saturday, Sunday 10am-5pm.

Staatliches Museum für Völkerkunde (Ethnological Museum).
42 Maximilianstraße.
Tel: 089/2285506.
Daily except Monday, 9.30am–4.30pm.

Städtische Galerie im Lenbachhaus.
33 Luisenstraße.
Tel: 089/521041.
Daily except Monday, 10am–6pm.

Valentin-Museum.
In Isartor Tower.
Tel: 089/223266.
Monday, Tuesday, Saturday, 11.01am–5.29pm; Sunday, 10.01am–5.29pm.

Villa Stuck.
60 Prinzregentenstraße, 8000, M80.
Tel: 089/4707086.
Daily, 10am–5pm.
Thursday, until 10.30pm.
Only open for special exhibitions.

ZAM (Centre for unusual museums).
26 Westenriederstraße.
Tel: 089/2914121.
Daily, 10am–6pm. Entrance: DM8

Advance Ticket Booking

Abendzeitung Hall.
79 Sendlinger Straße.
Tel: 089/7267024.

abr-Theaterkasse.
9 Neuhauser Straße (Haertle Passage).
Tel: 089/1204-0.

Kiosk in Marienplatz—Lower Level.
Tel: 089/229556.

Tickets for the Bavarian State Theatres only:

State Opera.
1 Maximilianstraße.
Tel: 089/221316.

Staatsschauspiel—State Theatre.
13 Maximilianstraße.
Tel: 089/225754.

Staatstheater am Gärtnerplatz.
Gärtnerplatz.
Tel: 089/2011328.

Kammerspiele Theatre.
26 Maximilianstraße.
Tel: 089/23721328.

Gasteig.
5 Rosenheimer Straße.
Tel: 089/748098–614.
Monday–Friday, 10.30am–2pm; 3–6pm; Saturday, 10.30am–2pm.

ART/PHOTO CREDITS

Director	**Hans Höfer**
Design Concept	**V Barl**
Cover Design	**Klaus Geisler**

PHOTOGRAPHY

8, 43, 75	**Gisela Albus**
9, 16, 19, 20, 22, 26, 30, 35, 36, 38, 48, 53, 56, 57, 58, 60, 62, 63, 64, 66, 69, 70, 71, 72, 83, 89, 92, 100, 104, 105, 107, 108, 109, 110, 111, 112, 114, 115, 117, 119	**Joachim Beust**
35, 77	**Willi Friedrich**
5, 18, 20, 31, 54, 71, 80	**Heinz Grosse**
87	**Wolfgang Koch**
3, 91, 93	**Alexander Laudien**
20, 42, 113	**Kurt Lehr**
23	**Loider Concept**
15, 27, 29, 33, 36, 44, 45, 48, 50, 51, 52, 56, 68 , 79, 95, 97, 101, 116	**Gisela Nicolaus**
6, 11, 13, 19, 20, 21, 28, 32, 37, 40, 41, 44, 46, 47 59, 67, 72, 73, 75, 78, 82, 83, 84, 85, 88, 102	**Gerd Pfeiffer**
55, 61, 74, 76, 89	**Regina Schmidt**
31, 34, 50, 54, 65, 81, 96, 98, 106	**Cliff Vestner**
14	**S Winkler Verlag**

ENGLISH EDITION

Translator	**Matthias Häcker**
Editor	**Elizabeth Boleman-Herring**
Production Editor	**Gareth Walters**
Managing Editor	**Christopher Catling**

Index

C

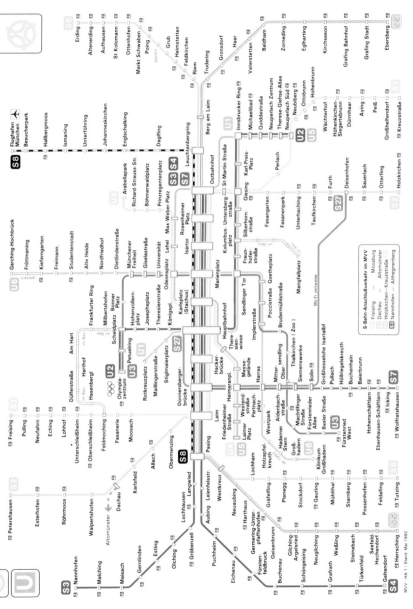

S-Bahnen im Münchner Verkehrs- und Tarifverbund

MVV · HA 1 / Stand: Mai 1992

INSIGHT GUIDES

COLORSET NUMBERS

You'll find the colorset number on the spine of each Insight Guide.

INSIGHT *POCKET* GUIDES

• •

United States: **Houghton Mifflin Company, Boston MA 02108**
Tel: (800) 2253362 Fax: (800) 4589501

Canada: **Thomas Allen & Son, 390 Steelcase Road East**
Markham, Ontario L3R 1G2
Tel: (416) 4759126 Fax: (416) 4756747

Great Britain: **GeoCenter UK, Hampshire RG22 4BJ**
Tel: (256) 817987 Fax: (256) 817988

Worldwide: **Höfer Communications Singapore 2262**
Tel: (65) 8612755 Fax: (65) 8616438

66 I was first drawn to the Insight Guides by the excellent "Nepal" volume. I can think of no book which so effectively captures the essence of a country. Out of these pages leaped the Nepal I know – the captivating charm of a people and their culture. I've since discovered and enjoyed the entire Insight Guide Series. Each volume deals with a country or city in the same sensitive depth, which is nowhere more evident than in the superb photography. 99

Sir Edmund Hillary